COOKING WITH CHEF DINOSAUR

By J. E. Nicks

First Edition

Jensen Publishing
16956 230th Avenue
Big Rapids, MI 49307
616-796-6637

ACKNOWLEDGMENTS

I would like to express my heartfelt thanks to the people who contributed to this cookbook. They include:

Jane Alexander
Miriam Cross
Marcheta Haile
Ruth Hamilton
JoAnn Harris
Mary Nicks
Susan Nicks
Pauline Ogden
Arlene Poel
Jane Roe
Mary Vivian
Linda Wininger

In Memory of:
Madeline Michelini
Maurice Ogden

A very special thanks to **Linda Wininger** whose art work and cover design are outstanding.

TABLE OF CONTENTS

ABOUT THIS COOKBOOK

This cookbook has an international flavor. For example, some of the countries represented in the Main Dish chapter are from America, China, Italy, Israel, Poland, Greece, and Indonesia, just to name a few. Many of these dishes are updated for the American style of cooking and include ingredients that are readily available.

This cookbook has been 20 years in the making and each recipe is kitchen-tested many times. There are many new and exciting recipes with over 16 new recipes cooking with fresh and dried fruit. Many of the recipes are low-calorie and low-fat, such as the Low-Fat Chicken Soup recipe on page 13. In the soup section, there are over 20 original recipes and a section on tips for soup making.

If you love to cook, and/or eat, and who doesn't, you will enjoy **Cooking with Chef Dinosaur.**

ABOUT CHEF DINOSAUR

You may be wondering about Chef Dinosaur. Many years ago, I lovingly nicknamed my husband The Last Dinosaur, as he is truly one-of-a-kind. He has been blessed with talents that most of us only dream of, and his contributions to society will influence people for generations to come.

Several years ago, as he was creating and experimenting with recipes in his kitchen, the name Chef Dinosaur was born. His cookbook, **Cooking with Chef Dinosaur**, is a serious cookbook with a humorous flair, a reflection of him. Enjoy!

-Mary Nicks

Soups

NOTES

FRENCH ONION SOUP

Serves 2

Why this is called French onion soup I can't tell you. The original recipe came from the Royal Palace in Brussels, Belgium and was made without onions, believe it or not!

3 medium onions, thinly sliced
1 - 14^1/$_2$ ounce can beef broth
^{1}/$_2$ cup cooking sherry
^{1}/$_4$ pound Gruyere cheese, grated
^{1}/$_4$ teaspoon fresh grated nutmeg
2 tablespoons olive oil
2 rusk biscuits
Pepper to taste

Saute the onions in the olive oil on very low heat until clear, stirring frequently. In a medium sized pot add onions, beef broth, nutmeg, and pepper. Simmer covered for 30 minutes.

Preheat the broiler. Add cooking sherry just before removing from burner. Ladle into heat proof serving bowls, top each with a rusk biscuit, and cover with cheese.

Place the heat proof bowls under the broiler (about 4 inches away) and heat until cheese is melted, bubbling and crisp.

Chef's Tip: This is a rich and hardy meal by itself or served with a salad. The cheese will be stringy but that is part of the fun. Eat it with a spoon, knife, and fork, or the best way you can!

POTATO SOUP

Serves 2

2 medium potatoes, peeled and diced
1/4 cup celery, finely diced
1/4 cup carrots, finely diced
1/4 cup onions, finely diced
1 teaspoon dried parsley
3 strips bacon, fried crisp and crumbled
1 - 5 ounce can condensed milk
1 - 14$\frac{1}{2}$ ounce can chicken broth
1 tablespoon cornstarch
4 tablespoons cold water
Salt and pepper to taste

Add celery and carrots to chicken broth, bring to a boil; reduce heat and simmer 10 minutes. Add potatoes, onions, and seasonings. Simmer 15 minutes, or until potatoes are cooked. Remove from heat.

Mix cornstarch with 4 tablespoons cold water. Add cornstarch to soup. Simmer until soup thickens, stirring continually. Remove from heat, add condensed milk. Simmer until warm. Serve with bacon on top and sprinkle with a pinch of parsley.

Chef's Tip: A nice garnish for Potato Soup is to add shredded cheddar cheese just before serving.

Serving Suggestion: Add 1 tablespoon sherry to each bowl. Or for a nice change of pace, add 1 - 8 ounce can of creamed corn while cooking.

CHILI, GROUND BEEF #1

Serves 4

1 tablespoon olive oil
1 pound ground beef, chuck or sirloin
1 large onion, diced
$^1/_2$ green pepper, diced
1 - 8 ounce can tomatoes
1 - 15 ounce can hot chili beans
$^1/_2$ cup ketchup
1 teaspoon chili powder
1 - 14$^1/_2$ ounce can beef broth
1 cup water
Salt and pepper to taste

Saute the ground beef until cooked. Drain to remove all the fat. Saute the onions and green pepper in a small amount of olive oil. Cut the tomatoes into small pieces. Combine all ingredients in a large pot and simmer for 1 hour.

Chef's Tip: Chili should be served with chopped onions, grated cheese, and crackers.

CHILI, GROUND BEEF #2

Serves 4

1 pound ground beef, chuck or sirloin
$1/2$ medium onion, diced
1 - 15 ounce can hot chili beans
1 - $14^{1}/_{2}$ ounce can beef broth
2 tablespoons cornstarch
$1/4$ cup ketchup
1 teaspoon chili powder
1 teaspoon cumin
$1/8$ teaspoon hot sauce or hot pepper
1 tablespoon mustard, dijon style
Salt and pepper to taste

Saute ground beef until cooked. Drain to remove all fat. Saute onions until tender. Add cornstarch and a small amount of beef broth and mix. Add all ingredients except cornstarch mixture. On a low burner bring to simmer. Add cornstarch and stir in. Simmer for 30 minutes, let rest for at least 2 hours before serving.

Chef's Tip: For a different flavor, add 1 - 15 ounce can of chili. This gives the chili a different but very good flavor.

CHILI, BEEF #3

Serves 4

1 pound sirloin, cubed into ¹/₂ inch cubes
3 cups water
1 large onion, diced
Olive oil, small amount
1 - 14 ounce can hot chili beans
1 - 14¹/₂ ounce can beef broth
¹/₂ cup ketchup
1 heaping teaspoon chili powder
¹/₂ teaspoon cumin
2 cloves garlic, finely chopped
Salt and pepper to taste

Bring the water to a boil in a large pot, add beef and simmer until tender, about 1¹/₂ hours.

Saute the onions in a small amount of olive oil, until the onions are clear. Set aside. When the meat is tender, remove from the pot, discard the broth and clean the pot. (The beef broth can be used if strained through cheesecloth several times.)

Add remaining ingredients and simmer for 1 hour. Remove from heat and let stand 1 hour, then reheat and serve.

Chef's Tip: Chili can be served with hot sauce, chopped onions, and grated cheese.

CHILI, BEEF #4

1 pound beef, trimmed and cubed
1 small onion, chopped
1 garlic clove, finely chopped
1 - 14 ounce can hot chili beans
$^{1}/_{4}$ teaspoon cayenne pepper
1 teaspoon chili powder
$^{1}/_{2}$ teaspoon cumin
2 tablespoons cornstarch
$^{1}/_{4}$ cup ketchup
Salt and pepper to taste

Place the beef in a large soup pan, cover with water and cook on low heat for 1 hour or until beef is tender. Remove beef with a slotted spoon. Strain broth twice through cheesecloth, or once through a coffee filter. Wash the pan with soap and water.

Mix the cornstarch in a small amount of water. Add the remaining ingredients and simmer for 30 minutes. Let chili rest for at least 2 hours. Reheat and serve with grated cheese and chopped raw onions. Garlic bread also makes a nice addition.

Chef's Tip: Cayenne pepper is a healthy addition because it promotes better circulation.

LOW-FAT CHICKEN SOUP

Serves 6
109 calories per serving

This chicken soup is very low in calories and also very low in fat.

2 chicken breasts, skinned
1 cup carrots, sliced
1 cup celery and leaves, sliced
2 cups spinach, chopped (optional)
1 1/2 cups cabbage, chopped
2 cups fresh mushrooms, sliced

1 medium onion, diced
1 - 14 ounce can chicken broth
1 tablespoon dried parsley
1 tablespoon fine herbs
3 cups water
Pepper to taste

Place chicken in a large pot with 3 cups water. Bring to a boil and simmer until chicken is cooked, about 20 minutes. Remove the chicken to cool. Strain the chicken broth into another pot. Clean the large pot and place chicken broth back into the pot along with the can of chicken broth.

When the chicken breasts are cool, remove from the bones and cut into 1/2 inch cubes. Bring broth to a boil; add carrots and celery, and simmer for 15 minutes. Add remaining ingredients and chicken; simmer for 15 minutes or until done. Let soup rest for at least 1 hour, then reheat and serve.

Chef's Tip: For regular chicken soup, omit the cabbage and substitute egg noodles. If you are counting protein servings, don't add the chicken with other ingredients. Weigh individual portions and add to single serving of soup when it is reheated.

NAVY BEAN SOUP

Serves 4

1 pound small navy beans
1 - 10 ounce package of smoky links, cut in $^1/_4$ inch pieces
$^1/_2$ cup onions, chopped
$^1/_2$ cup carrots, finely diced
$^1/_2$ cup celery with leaves, finely diced
1 - 14$^1/_2$ ounce can chicken broth
1 tablespoon parsley or fine herbs
$^1/_2$ teaspoon hot sauce
Salt and pepper to taste

Soak beans overnight in a large pot of water. Discard water and rinse beans. Add chicken broth and enough water to cover the beans by one inch. Add remaining ingredients except smoky links. Bring to a boil, then simmer until beans are almost tender. Remove from heat, spoon out 1$^1/_2$ cups of soup and run through a blender to puree; then add to the soup. Add smoky links. Cook for 15 minutes and correct the seasoning.

Chef's Tip: Let the soup rest for at least 1 hour before reheating to serve.

Serving Suggestion: Serve with corn bread Johnny cakes or muffins, chopped onions, and hot sauce.

SPINACH SOUP

Serves 2

5 ounces spinach, chopped and cooked
1 - 14^1/$_2$ ounce can chicken broth
1 teaspoon cornstarch
4 tablespoons cold water
^{1}/$_8$ teaspoon fresh ground nutmeg
1 - 5 ounce can condensed milk
Salt and pepper to taste

Place spinach and ^{1}/$_2$ can chicken broth in a blender and puree until smooth. Place remainder of the chicken broth in a saucepan and also add blender ingredients. Add salt, pepper, and nutmeg; bring to a full boil.

Mix cornstarch in cold water and add to soup. When soup is thickened, remove from heat. Add about ^{1}/$_2$ can of condensed milk. Reduce heat and warm soup, but do not boil. Serve with croutons.

Chef's Tip: A small amount of chopped ham can be added after the blender step.

CORN CHOWDER

Serves 4 - 6

2 smoked pork chops, diced (fat trimmed first)
1 - 8 ounce can creamed corn
1 - 8 ounce can corn, not drained
1 - 8 ounce can stewed tomatoes, chopped
1 small onion, diced
1 - 14½ ounce can chicken broth or stock
1 tablespoon parsley
4 ounces sharp cheddar cheese, grated
1 - 5 ounce can condensed milk or heavy cream
2 medium potatoes, diced
2 tablespoons cornstarch
4 tablespoons cold water
2 tablespoons white cooking wine
Salt and pepper to taste

Saute pork chops until well heated, add onions and saute until clear; set aside. Cook potatoes in chicken broth until tender. Add corn and tomatoes, simmer 10 minutes.

Add pork chops, onions, and parsley. Add salt and pepper to taste. Add cheese and melt.

Mix water and cornstarch, then add to soup mixture. Remove from heat, add wine and condensed milk; simmer until hot but not boiling. Ladle into bowls and garnish with fresh parsley. Serve with rye bread.

YELLOW SPLIT PEA SOUP

Serves 6

Many people don't like the taste of green pea soup. Yellow peas
have a different taste. Try this one.

1 cup yellow split peas
1 - 14$^1/_2$ ounce can beef broth
1 medium onion, diced
2 medium carrots, finely diced
$^1/_2$ pound cooked ham, finely diced
$^1/_4$ cup cooking sherry
1 tablespoon dried parsley flakes, or 2 tablespoons fresh parsley
Salt and pepper to taste

Soak the peas overnight in 3 cups of water. Pour off any excess
water. Add 2 cups fresh water and beef broth. Add the onions,
carrots, sherry, parsley, and salt and pepper. Simmer until the
carrots and peas are soft, about an hour. Add the ham and simmer
for 10 minutes. Remove from the burner and let rest 1 hour, then
reheat and serve.

Chef's Tip: Smoked pork chops can be substituted for ham. This
recipe makes a light soup. If you like a more full bodied soup, try
this suggestion. Add an extra cup of peas. Halfway through the
cooking process, remove 1 cup of peas and blend in a blender until
smooth. Add to soup mixture. This is an easy way to thicken the
soup.

AUNT JANE'S TOMATO SOUP

Serves 4 - 6

This old Polish soup recipe dates back about 50 years. You must try it! It turns a can of soup into something that's wonderful. This recipe was furnished by Jane Roe of Livonia, Michigan. Jane is a very dear friend, and has been for over 40 years.

1 beef shank with bone
2 quarts water
1 bay leaf
1 cup carrots, chopped
1 onion, chopped
1 parsley root about $1/4$ inch diameter, 2 inches long
1 celery stalk, sliced into $1/2$ inch pieces
1 - $10^3/4$ ounce can tomato soup
$1/2$ pint half-and-half or cream
1 tablespoon flour

Soak beef in water for an hour. Rinse, add clean water, let meat come to a boil. Rinse, add clean water (2 quarts). Add bay leaf and onion, simmer until meat is almost tender.

Add carrots, celery, and parsley root. Cook until carrots and celery are tender. Remove parsley root. Remove meat, add the tomato soup, bring to a simmer.

Mix $1/2$ pint of half-and-half (or cream) with 1 tablespoon flour. Add warm soup to this mixture, about $1/2$ cup. Add back to the soup and let soup come to a simmer. Serve with dark bread.

18

VEGETABLE BEEF SOUP

Serves 6

1 medium onion, diced
1 pound lean beef, ½ inch cubes
1 - 8½ ounce can corn
1 - 8½ ounce can tomatoes
1 cup carrots, diced
1 cup celery, sliced
1 cup potatoes, diced
1 - 14½ ounce can beef broth

1 teaspoon fine herbs
1 teaspoon dried parsley
Salt and pepper to taste
2 tablespoons cornstarch mixed with ¼ cup cold water
1 teaspoon sugar
1 teaspoon Kitchen Bouquet®

In a large pot place 3 cups of water and bring to a boil. Reduce heat to a simmer and add beef. Cook the beef until tender, about 1 hour or more. Remove the meat and rinse with cold water. Strain broth twice, once in a course strainer and once in a very fine strainer. Clean the pot.

Add the beef broth, beef, onions, carrots, celery, and potatoes. Bring to a boil; reduce heat to a simmer and cook for 30 minutes. Add remaining ingredients and simmer for 30 minutes. Let the soup rest for at least 1 hour before serving.

Chef's Tip: Almost any cut of beef will work well, but I use a sirloin cut which works best. Almost any combination of vegetables can be used. For example, try adding 1 cup of spinach. Another variation is to add mixed beans. These can be cooked separately and added after the carrots and potatoes are cooked. If you like your soup more spicy, try adding 1 teaspoon of garlic chips and ½ cup ketchup. The sugar can be omitted if tomatoes are not used. Taste the soup several times during the cooking process, but don't make any corrections until the soup is finished.

CLAM CHOWDER

Serves 2

2 medium potatoes, peeled and diced
1 small onion, peeled and chopped
1 - 8 ounce can baby clams, drained and rinsed
1 - 5 ounce can condensed milk
4 tablespoons water
1 teaspoon dried mustard
$^1/_8$ teaspoon tarragon
1 tablespoon plus cornstarch
2 tablespoons white wine

Mix the last 5 ingredients (water, dried mustard, tarragon, cornstarch, and white wine) and set aside. Cover the potatoes just barely with water. Cook potatoes until half done, about 10 minutes. Add onions and clams. Cook on simmer until onions are clear. Stir in cornstarch mixture and cook until the chowder thickens. Remove from heat and stir in most of the condensed milk.

Serving Suggestion: This is a hardy chowder. Serve with corn bread Johnny cakes.

LIMA BEAN SOUP

Serves 6

2 cups baby limas or large lima beans
1 - 14^1/$_2$ ounce can chicken broth
1 cup meat, diced (ham, polish sausage, roast pork)
^{1}/$_8$ teaspoon garlic chips
^{1}/$_2$ cup celery with leaves, finely chopped
^{1}/$_2$ cup onions, chopped
^{1}/$_2$ cup carrots, diced
^{1}/$_2$ teaspoon fine herbs
1 tablespoon parsley flakes, dried
Salt and pepper to taste

Rinse beans and let soak overnight. Add chicken broth and enough water to cover beans by 1 inch. Bring to a boil and simmer until beans are half cooked. Add additional water as necessary.

Add garlic chips, celery, onions, carrots, fine herbs, and parsley, but not the meat. Simmer until carrots are almost tender and remove from heat. Ladle out 2 cups of the mixture and blend in a blender. Add mixture back to soup and add meat. Simmer for 15 minutes, then remove from heat and let rest for 1 hour. Reheat and serve.

Chef's Tip: For a tang, add about ^{1}/$_4$ cup ketchup to the soup and several drops of hot sauce. Bean soup should be served with hot sauce and chopped raw onions. Bean soup can also be served with corn bread Johnny cakes. This is a meal in itself and the leftovers are great.

CREAM OF ASPARAGUS SOUP

Serves 2

We have a small asparagus patch in our backyard. Every spring when the fresh young asparagus comes up we have this soup as a main meal several times.

$^1/_2$ pound asparagus (about 10 or 12 stalks)
1 - 14$^1/_2$ ounce can chicken broth
1 - 5 ounce can condensed (evaporated) milk
$^1/_4$ teaspoon fresh nutmeg, grated
4 strips bacon, diced
2 cups water
$^1/_4$ cup onions, chopped

Bring water to a boil and cook asparagus for 3 minutes. Remove from heat, drain and cut asparagus tips off. Fry bacon until crisp, drain on paper towel. Arrange bacon and asparagus tips in serving bowls.

Place asparagus stalks in the same pan, add chicken broth and nutmeg. Simmer 10 minutes. Remove from heat and run through a blender. Return mixture to a pan and heat until hot but not boiling. Add condensed milk and cook 3 or 4 minutes. Ladle into soup bowls and serve.

Chef's Tip: Leftovers can be warmed in the microwave.

CREAM OF BROCCOLI SOUP

Serves 2

If you don't know what to do with that leftover broccoli, try this recipe. I don't even like broccoli, but this light soup is wonderful. It's a perfect way to start a meal.

1 - 14^1/2 ounce can chicken broth or fresh broth
2 cups broccoli buds, chopped
1 small onion, chopped
1 teaspoon horseradish
^{1}/2 teaspoon Italian seasoning
1 tablespoon cornstarch
2 tablespoons water
2 - 3 ounces heavy cream or condensed milk
Salt and pepper to taste
Parsley for garnish

Cook the broccoli and onions in the chicken broth until tender. Add seasonings and simmer for 5 minutes. Blend in a blender until smooth. Mix cornstarch and 2 tablespoons water and add to the soup. Cook until the soup thickens; remove from the heat and stir in cream or milk. Ladle into hot bowls and garnish with parsley.

MANHATTAN CLAM CHOWDER

Serves 4

1 - 8 ounce bottle of clam juice
1 - 10 ounce can of baby clams
$^1/_2$ small onion, chopped
1 - 8 ounce can tomatoes
$^1/_8$ cup ketchup
2 small potatoes
2 level tablespoons white sugar
2 level tablespoons of flour mixed with
4 tablespoons water
Several drops of hot sauce
Salt and pepper to taste

Trim and dice the potatoes into small pieces. In a soup pot, add all ingredients except the clams and flour mixture. Bring to a boil and simmer for another 20 minutes. Add the clams and flour mixture; stir until the soup thickens. Let the chowder rest for at least 1 hour, then reheat.

Chef's Tip: The baby clams can be purchased at Wal-Mart® or K-Mart®. If baby clams are not available, use a 6 ounce can of minced clams.

Salads

NOTES

PASTA SALAD

Serves 2

1 cup pasta
2 tablespoons onion, chopped
2 tablespoons green onions, chopped
4 tablespoons celery, chopped
Salt and pepper to taste

Cook the pasta in salted water until tender but still firm, drain well. Any of the five dressings below can be used, depending on your taste.

Dressings:

3 tablespoons lemon juice
3 tablespoons oil
$^1/_4$ teaspoon dry mustard
$^1/_4$ teaspoon fine herbs

$^1/_4$ cup mayonnaise
$^1/_4$ cup yogurt
$^1/_4$ teaspoon fine herbs
$^1/_4$ teaspoon dry mustard

$^1/_4$ cup mayonnaise
$^1/_4$ cup raspberry vinegar
$^1/_4$ teaspoon garlic powder
$^1/_2$ teaspoon sugar

$^1/_4$ cup mayonnaise
$^1/_4$ cup buttermilk
$^1/_4$ teaspoon dry mustard
$^1/_4$ teaspoon garlic powder

$^1/_4$ cup raspberry vinegar
$^1/_8$ cup oil
$^1/_4$ cup white wine

BEAN SALAD

Serves 2 - 4

This recipe is low-calorie, high-fiber and very low-fat.

1 - 15 ounce can pinto beans
$^1/_8$ cup seasoned vinegar
1 teaspoon dijon mustard
Several drops of hot sauce
$^1/_8$ cup onions, chopped
3 tablespoons sweet and spicy salad dressing
1 teaspoon sugar
Salt and pepper to taste

Drain and rinse the beans. Add onions to the beans. Mix the remaining ingredients very well. Mix the sauce into the beans.

Chef's Tip: Any variety of beans can be used. Also, chopped celery can be added. This dish can be refrigerated but I think it is better at room temperature.

TUNA SALAD

Serves 2

1 - 6 ounce can tuna, well drained
1 hard boiled egg, chopped
3 tablespoons onions, chopped
1 tablespoon sweet relish
Salt and pepper to taste
2 heaping tablespoons mayonnaise

Mix all ingredients; dust the top with paprika. Refrigerate to let the flavors blend.

Serving Suggestion: This tuna salad can be served on a bed of lettuce or in a sandwich.

COLE SLAW

Serves 2

1½ cups cabbage, finely shredded
½ onion, finely diced
1 carrot, shredded
½ teaspoon celery seeds
4 tablespoons cole slaw dressing

Mix all ingredients; dust with paprika. Refrigerate for at least 1 hour to let ingredients blend.

Chef's Tip: If you don't have cole slaw dressing, blend together ½ cup mayonnaise plus ¼ cup white vinegar.

Serving Suggestion: For a change, try adding raisins and/or walnuts just before serving. Diced apples also make another nice addition.

PICKLED BEETS

1 - 16 ounce can of sliced beets, drained
$^1/_2$ cup white vinegar
$^1/_2$ cup water
$^1/_8$ cup sugar
$^1/_8$ cup honey
$^1/_2$ teaspoon pickling spices
$^1/_2$ teaspoon salt
1 garlic clove, chopped
$^1/_8$ teaspoon hot pepper flakes

Add all ingredients except beets and bring to a boil. Remove from the heat and let cool. Place the beets in the pint jar and cover with the pickling juice. Place in the refrigerator for 1 week.

Chef's Tip: You may wish to cover the jar with plastic wrap before screwing down the lid. This will keep the lid from coming in contact with the vinegar.

CARROTS AND RAISINS

Serves 2

1 cup shredded carrots
$1/4$ cup raisins
$1/4$ cup chopped nuts (walnuts or almonds)
$1/4$ cup grapefruit juice
2 tablespoons honey

Mix the honey and grapefruit juice well. Mix all ingredients.

Chef's Tip: You may have to microwave the grapefruit juice and honey for 10 seconds to melt the honey.

ASPARAGUS SALAD

Serves 2

1/2 pound fresh asparagus, stalks trimmed
1 teaspoon sesame seeds
1 tablespoon cooking oil
3 tablespoons raspberry vinegar
Salt and pepper to taste

Blanch the asparagus in boiling water for 2 minutes, then place in cold water to stop the cooking. Pat dry on paper towels. Cut into bite size pieces. Mix the salt, pepper, oil, and vinegar. Toss the asparagus, sesame seeds, and vinegar mixture until well coated.

WALDORF SALAD

This is not the original Waldorf recipe from the Waldorf Hotel. I remember some 30 years ago a woman was having lunch at the Waldorf and liked their salad. She asked for the recipe which was freely given to her. Upon request, she left her name and address and when she arrived home, she was stunned to find an enormous invoice from the Waldorf Hotel. She had to pay it.

1 large tart red apple
3 tablespoons golden raisins
3 tablespoons walnut halves
3 tablespoons shredded coconut (sweet)
1 teaspoon lemon juice
1 tablespoon salad dressing or mayonnaise
2 tablespoons yogurt

Cut the apple into cubes. Mix the apple in the lemon juice to prevent apples from browning. Mix the salad dressing and yogurt. Mix all ingredients to coat. Dust the top with cinnamon. Chill in the refrigerator before serving.

SPINACH AND FETA SALAD

Serves 2

5 ounces fresh spinach, washed and trimmed
2 ounces feta cheese, crumbled
2 tablespoons onions, chopped
2 tablespoons carrots, shredded
1 tablespoon cooking oil
3 tablespoons rice wine
Salt and pepper to taste

Pat the spinach dry with paper towels. Cut the spinach into bite size pieces. Mix the cooking oil and rice wine. Toss all ingredients until well coated.

Chef's Tip: Olive oil is the best application for this salad; however, a general cooking oil such as vegetable oil will also work well.

35

EGG SALAD

Serves 2

This egg salad recipe can be served on toast or on a bed of lettuce for a light lunch.

2 hard boiled eggs
1 tablespoon sweet relish, drained
2 tablespoons onions, chopped
1 tablespoon salad mustard
3 tablespoons mayonnaise
Salt and pepper to taste

Peel and chop the eggs. Mix all ingredients. Dust with paprika.

Chef's Tip: A few drops of hot sauce can be added for tang. Also, 1 teaspoon of horseradish can also be added.

STUFFED AVOCADO

Serves 2

1 avocado
¼ tart apple, chopped
10 seedless grapes, halved
1 tablespoon yogurt
1 tablespoon mayonnaise
1 teaspoon lemon juice
Salt and pepper to taste

Cut the avocado in half, seed, and spoon out the fruit into bite size pieces. Mix all ingredients and fill avocado halves. Sprinkle paprika on top for color.

Chef's Tip: If you add a small banana and some cooked chicken, you have a dish from Bolivia.

FRUIT AND FIVE-SPICE POWDER

Serves 4

1 - 8 ounce can chunk pineapple, not drained
1 orange, peeled and sliced
1 red tart apple, sliced
8 ounces seedless grapes
1 firm banana, sliced
Five-spice powder to taste

Mix all fruit together. Make sure the apple and banana are well coated with fruit juices. Sprinkle the five-spice powder on top and serve.

Chef's Tip: Any fresh or canned fruit, such as pears, grapefruit, or peaches, can be used in this dish. It's the five-spice powder that does the trick. Five-spice powder is a Chinese spice that can be found in most grocery stores or Middle East shops. Five-spice powder is made from fennel, star anise, red pepper, licorice, and cloves.

STUFFED MUSHROOMS

Serves 2

4 large mushrooms
1 tablespoon white cooking wine
1 tablespoon chopped onions
1 teaspoon seasoned vinegar
$\frac{1}{8}$ teaspoon sweet relish
2 teaspoons seasoned bread crumbs
4 cashews
1 tablespoon honey dijon dressing
1 tablespoon cheddar cheese, finely chopped
Butter
1 tablespoon french dressing

Note: This recipe makes four stuffed mushrooms in two varieties.

Cut the mushrooms around the stem and pop out the stem. Chop the stems finely and saute in 1 tablespoon of white wine until all liquid is absorbed. Remove from heat and divide into two bowls. Put a little butter on your fingers and rub on the outside of each mushroom.

Recipe #1:
Saute the onions in the seasoned vinegar until clear. Add onions, relish, 1 teaspoon of bread crumbs, and french dressing, then mix. Add to the first bowl. Divide the mixture and spoon into two mushrooms.

Recipe #2:
Chop the cashews very fine; add to bowl 2. Add 1 teaspoon of bread crumbs and 1 tablespoon of honey dijon dressing. Mix well and spoon into the remaining two mushrooms. Preheat the oven to 375°. Dot all four mushrooms with the cheese. Bake for 15 minutes and serve hot.

Continued on next page

Cooking notes about mushrooms:
When cleaning mushrooms never wash them. Either use a mushroom brush or wipe with a moist kitchen towel. Mushrooms are one of the most versatile of all foods. They are like onions and can be added to almost any dish. They make a good addition to soups, stews, omelettes, and steak.

When cooking mushrooms use as little oil or butter as possible because they act as a blotter, absorbing all liquid. Mushrooms are 50% water and will give up most of the water during the cooking process. For this reason I rub the mushroom with a little butter to hold the moisture in.

Mushrooms can be stuffed with almost any combination of ingredients. Shown below is a partial listing of good additions to mushrooms. Experiment and try your own combinations. Experience the creative part of cooking.

Liver, Cooked Sausage, Shrimp, Clams, Cream Cheese, Cheddar Cheese, Oysters, Crab Meat, Chicken, Ham, Spinach, Eggs, Anchovies, Capers, Olives, Nuts, Avocado, Onions

Mushrooms will accept a variety of seasonings, to name a few:

Salt, Pepper, Mustard, Wine, Parsley, Fine Herbs, Mint, Ground Ginger, Chives, Celery Seeds

MADELINE'S ANTIPASTO

Serves 4

Jane Alexander, a very dear family friend, furnished this recipe in memory of her special Grandmother-in-law, Madeline Michelini. Antipasto is the Italian word meaning before food, or hors d'oeuvre.

Sauce:

½ cup wine vinegar
⅔ cup olive oil
2 - 6 ounce cans of tomato sauce
Salt and pepper to taste

Antipasto:

Jar of cocktail onions, drained
Celery, sliced
Cauliflower, cut up
Green pepper, sliced
Small mushrooms
Carrots, sliced

Green beans, sliced
Black olives
Green olives
1 can albacore tuna in water, drained
1 can sardines, drained

Heat wine vinegar, olive oil, tomato sauce, salt, and pepper in heavy pan. In a separate pan, fry the remaining ingredients lightly in 1 tablespoon of heated olive oil for 1 minute. Combine the ingredients with the vinegar/oil/tomato sauce. Serve hot or cold.

Chef's Note: A small can of anchovies can be added to this classic Italian salad for more zest. See pages 143 and 144 for more of Madeline's recipes.

POTATO SALAD

4 large boiling potatoes
$1/4$ cup onion, chopped
$1/4$ cup celery, chopped
1 hard cooked egg, chopped
Salt and pepper to taste
$1/2$ teaspoon celery seeds
1 tablespoon sweet relish
1 tablespoon salad mustard
$3/4$ cup mayonnaise
$1/2$ cup cheddar cheese, diced (optional)

Peel, dice, and boil potatoes until tender. Drain well and blot with paper towels. Mix sweet relish, mustard, and mayonnaise. Blend all ingredients well and dust the top with paprika.

Chef's Tip: Canned potatoes can be substituted (2 - 16 ounce cans are required). Be sure to drain well and blot dry with paper towels.

SALMON SALAD

This is a light dish, ideal for summer time.

1 - 6 ounce can of red salmon, well drained
2 tablespoons onion, chopped
2 tablespoons celery, finely chopped
3 tablespoons mayonnaise or salad dressing
1 teaspoon sweet relish
Salt and pepper to taste
1 tomato, quartered
Lettuce leaves
Garlic powder, optional

Mix all ingredients except the tomato and lettuce. Serve on a bed of lettuce leaves and garnish with tomato wedges.

ALMOND AND ORANGE SALAD

Serves 4

1 small can Mandarin oranges, well drained
1 envelope unflavored gelatine (makes 2 cups liquid)
³/₄ cup water
¹/₄ cup sugar
³/₄ cup boiling water
1 - 5 ounce can condensed milk
¹/₂ teaspoon vanilla extract
¹/₂ teaspoon almond extract

Measure the cold water into a bowl. Add the gelatin and let stand
for 1 or 2 minutes. Add sugar to the mixture. Pour boiling water
into a bowl; stir in gelatin mixture.

Combine milk, vanilla, and almond. Add to the gelatin mixture
along with the oranges. Transfer to a glass baking dish and
refrigerate until firm.

Chef's Tip: This is a very light salad that goes well with any
Chinese dish.

Main Dishes

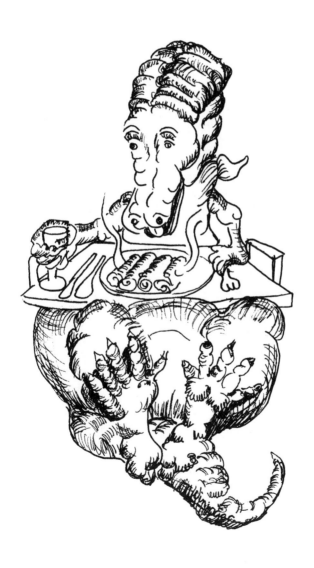

NOTES

SPICY CHICKEN

Serves 4

Spicy chicken is a very easy recipe to fix. It has a wonderful flavor and is inexpensive. What more could you ask for?

4 - 6 chicken thighs or legs
1 - 6 ounce can tomato paste
8 ounces beer
2 tablespoons Picante sauce
$^1/_2$ teaspoon dry mustard
1 garlic clove, chopped
2 tablespoons brown sugar
2 tablespoons vinegar, white or cider
1 tablespoon Worcestershire® sauce
$^1/_2$ teaspoon celery seeds
Several drops of hot sauce (optional)
Salt and pepper to taste

Brown the chicken in a little oil, remove and spoon off all oil. Mix the remaining ingredients. Place chicken and sauce in a heavy sauce pan, cover and cook 45 minutes on low heat.

Chef's Tip: Browning the chicken helps cook the fat out. Also, the skin can be removed, if desired.

Serving Suggestion: Serve with cooked noodles and a green vegetable.

GREEK STYLE BEEF AND ONIONS

Serves 4

This recipe is from Greece. Most countries from that region use allspice as a seasoning. Nutmeg is another commonly used seasoning.

1 pound lean beef (sirloin or round steak)
    trimmed of fat and cubed into 1-inch pieces
1 large onion, sliced
1 - 8 ounce can tomato sauce
1 cup red cooking wine
Salt and pepper to taste
1 large clove garlic, chopped
$1/2$ teaspoon allspice
$1/2$ teaspoon sugar
1 cinnamon stick (2-inches)
$1/8$ teaspoon hot sauce

Brown the beef well in a frying pan. Mix everything else except onions and beef. Place beef and onions in a large pot, add sauce and simmer 2 hours or more, until beef is very tender. Serve with rice, noodles, or macaroni.

Chef's Tip: This is an ideal dish for a slow cooker. If you don't have one, it is well worth the purchase price because so many dishes can be slow cooked and beef is really tender. Cooking time in a slow cooker is about 5 hours, unattended. On a Sunday afternoon, take in a movie while dinner is being slow cooked. Another tip is to mix several tablespoons of Parmesan or grated Greek cheese into the rice or noodles, just before serving.

SHRIMP EGG FU YUNG

Makes 4 Pancakes

Most Egg Fu Yung recipes call for a chicken broth, but this one uses beef broth. You have to try it to see how good it is.

Sauce:
$^3/_4$ cup beef broth
3 tablespoons cooking sherry
2 teaspoons cornstarch
Salt and seasoned pepper to taste
Several drops of Kitchen Bouquet®

Mix the cornstarch in the sherry to dissolve. Heat the other ingredients to a boil. Add sherry and stir until thickened. Remove to a low burner to remain hot.

Egg Fu Yung:
1 cup cooked shrimp, chopped in quarters
1 cup bean sprouts, fresh
3 eggs, beaten
1 tablespoon soy sauce
3 tablespoons onions, finely chopped
1 tablespoon cooking oil
2 or 3 pea pods, finely chopped or 2 green onions, finely chopped
Cooking oil

Saute onions and pea pods (or green onions) in 1 tablespoon cooking oil until clear. Set aside to cool. Mix all ingredients well. Add 1 teaspoon cooking oil to a 4-inch frying pan and bring to medium heat. Ladle in $^1/_2$ cup of the Egg Fu Yung mixture. Cook until brown, turn, and cook the other side. Remove to a well heated plate. Make the remaining pancakes. Serve with hot boiled rice.

Chef's Tip: The reason for letting the onions cool is not to add hot onions to the egg mixture.

Variations: Cooked chicken or pork can be substituted for the shrimp. If pork is used shred into fine slices.

49

SMOKED PORK CHOPS AND CHERRIES

Serves 2

2 smoked pork chops, fat trimmed
$1/2$ cup frozen sweet cherries
2 tablespoons frozen orange juice concentrate
3 tablespoons water
$1/2$ teaspoon cornstarch plus 1 tablespoon water
$1/8$ teaspoon cinnamon
Pinch ground nutmeg
Pinch ground cloves

Cut the cherries in half. While the pork chops are being broiled or grilled, mix the cornstarch in 1 tablespoon of water. Add all sauce ingredients to a saucepan and bring to a light boil. Add the cornstarch and water to thicken. Remove the pork chops to a heated plate and serve the cherries on the side.

Chef's Tip: This sauce also works well over broiled or grilled chicken breasts.

FRENCH STUFFED ZUCCHINI

Serves 2

Zucchini lovers: this is a low-fat and low-calorie dish.

1 medium to large zucchini
$^1/_4$ pound ground beef
$^1/_4$ cup onion, chopped
$^1/_4$ cup rice, cooked
Salt and pepper to taste
$^1/_4$ teaspoon ground nutmeg
1 garlic clove, finely chopped
$^1/_2$ cup ketchup
1 teaspoon horseradish
3 tablespoons cooking wine

Cut the zucchini in half and spoon out the center. Chop into small, bite size pieces. Brown the ground beef, drain or spoon off all fat. Brown the onions. Mix the zucchini, ground beef, onion, rice, salt, pepper, nutmeg, and garlic. Add the wine and mix.

Spoon into the zucchini shells. Mix the ketchup and horseradish. Spoon over the top of the zucchini shells. Place in a baking dish and bake covered for 50 minutes in a 350° oven.

LAMB PATTIES WITH APRICOTS

Serves 2

You will just have to trust me with this one. Lamb, apricots, and cranberry juice do go well together.

2 lamb patties
6 dried apricots
3 tablespoons white wine
$^3/_4$ cup cranberry juice
1 teaspoon sugar
1 tablespoon cornstarch plus 2 tablespoons water
Pinch of cinnamon

Slice the apricots very thinly and let soak in the white wine for several hours. While the lamb patties are being broiled or grilled, mix the sugar, cornstarch, and cinnamon well. Add the apricots and cook over low heat until thickened. Serve the apricot sauce on the side.

Chef's Tip: This sauce also goes well with pork.

Serving Suggestion: Serve with boiled potatoes.

VEAL CHOPS AND APRICOT BRANDY

Serves 2

2 center cut veal chops
2 green onions, finely chopped with the greens

Sauce:
$^1/_4$ cup apricot brandy
$^1/_4$ cup tomato sauce
$^1/_4$ cup condensed milk
Salt and pepper to taste
1 egg yolk
$^1/_4$ teaspoon tarragon leaves
$^1/_4$ teaspoon rosemary (crumbled)
1 teaspoon cornstarch mixed in 2 tablespoons water

Saute the chops on both sides in 2 tablespoons cooking oil for 4 minutes each.

Mix the remaining ingredients in a saucepan and cook until thickened. Remove the chops to a heated serving dish. Top with sauce and green onions.

Chef's Tip: The sauce may not have to be thickened. It depends on how much you are making. Add the cornstarch and water last, as you may not need any at all.

Serving Suggestion: Serve with hot buttered noodles.

POACHED FISH AND HONEY SAUCE

Serves 2

2 salmon steaks
1 cup chicken broth
1 teaspoon fine herbs
2 onion slices
1 cup water
Salt and pepper to taste

Mix chicken broth, herbs, onion, water, salt, and pepper and bring to a simmer or light boil. Cook the salmon 12 minutes per inch of thickness, turning once. Remove to a hot serving dish.

Sauce:
2 tablespoons honey
1 tablespoon mustard, dijon style
1 tablespoon lemon juice

Combine all ingredients and serve with the fish.

Chef's Tip: Broiling fish dries it out. Fish cooked with this method leaves it light but moist.

STUFFED TURKEY

Serves 2

1 small turkey breast fillet (approximately ½ pound)
5 or 6 dried apricots
¼ cup white cooking wine
1 cup seasoned croutons
1 teaspoon parsley
1 cup chicken broth
1 teaspoon Kitchen Bouquet®
Salt and pepper to taste

Soak the apricots in the wine overnight. Mix the croutons, parsley, salt, pepper, and chicken broth. Cut a pocket into the turkey fillet and stuff with the stuffing. Rub the Kitchen Bouquet® over the turkey. Place the turkey and stuffing in a baking dish, cover with aluminum foil and bake in a 350° oven for 45 minutes. Remove and spoon sauce over the turkey.

Chef's Tip: Raisins and nuts work well as a stuffing for the turkey. Also, orange liqueur can be used rather than white wine.

RIBS IN WINE

Serves 2

This rib dish has the flavor of dry white wine and is tender and delicious.

1 pound spare ribs (pork or beef)
1 bottle dry white table wine
Your favorite barbecue sauce

Simmer the ribs in a heavy saucepan in about a half a bottle of wine for at least 2 hours. (The other half of the bottle of wine is for you!)

Broil the ribs on each side until crisp. Brush with barbecue sauce and serve.

GERMAN LIVER AND APPLES

Serves 2

Many people who don't like liver love this German dish because the apples change the flavor of the liver.

$^1/_2$ pound calves liver, thinly sliced
1 tart cooking apple, peeled and sliced
1 large potato, peeled and thinly sliced
1 cup chicken broth
Salt and pepper to taste
2 tablespoons flour
$^1/_2$ teaspoon sweet paprika (Hungarian style)
1 tablespoon cornstarch, dissolved in 2 tablespoons water

Dust the liver with flour and brown in 2 tablespoons cooking oil. Remove to a baking dish. Combine the chicken broth, salt, pepper, and paprika in a saucepan. When near boiling, add the cornstarch and water to thicken.

Layer the baking dish with liver, apples next, then potatoes. Spoon the sauce over the top and bake in a 350° oven about 50 minutes, or until the potatoes are cooked.

Chef's Tip: If you can't find calves liver, use beef liver. Soak the beef liver in milk for about 30 minutes. This will reduce the harsh beef flavor.

TURKEY LOAF

Serves 4

This low-calorie, low-fat dish almost tastes like a beef meat loaf when prepared this way.

1 pound ground turkey
$^1/_4$ cup bread crumbs, seasoned
$^1/_4$ cup grated Parmesan cheese
1 egg
1 tablespoon Kitchen Bouquet®
1 tablespoon steak sauce
1 teaspoon fine herbs
Salt and pepper to taste

Mix all ingredients very well by hand. Transfer to a glass baking loaf pan and bake in a 400° oven for 50 minutes.

SPICY CHICKEN LIVERS

Serves 2

This sounds like a hot, spicy dish; it isn't. Even if you don't like liver you will love these Spicy Chicken Livers! The original recipe was from Indonesia.

³/₄ pound chicken livers
¹/₂ cup bourbon or blended whiskey
1 teaspoon red pepper flakes
1 tablespoon hot sauce
1 cup flour, plus ¹/₃ cup Parmesan cheese, grated
Salt and pepper to taste
3 tablespoons fresh parsley, finely chopped
1 medium onion, sliced
¹/₂ lemon, cut in wedges
2 tablespoons white wine

Wash and trim fat from chicken livers. Cut large ones in half. Mix bourbon, red pepper flakes, and hot sauce. Add chicken livers and onions. Marinate in the refrigerator for at least 2 hours.

Remove livers from the refrigerator, separate the onions, and drain off the bourbon. In a double paper bag, add flour, grated Parmesan cheese, salt, pepper, and parsley. Add a few livers at a time to the bag and shake until well coated. Remove to wax paper. Repeat the process until all livers are coated.

Add 4 or 5 tablespoons oil to a frying pay, heat to medium-hot. Add one liver to test; the liver should begin to sizzle immediately. Add all livers and fry until crisp. Turn and fry on all sides. While livers are frying, place onion in a separate frying pan with 2 tablespoons white wine and saute until soft. Remove livers to a hot serving plate and garnish with lemon wedges and onions.

FLANK STEAK & PEANUT SAUCE

Serves 2

This dish is from Indonesia and can be made to your personal level of spiciness by adding or reducing the hot sauce.

To make Flank Steak:
$1/2$ pound flank steak
1 small onion, grated
1 garlic clove, minced
1 teaspoon coriander powder
1 teaspoon sugar
1 tablespoon red cooking wine
Salt and pepper to taste
1 teaspoon hot sauce
1 teaspoon ginger

Slice flank steak across the grain into $1/8$ inch slices. Mix all ingredients; add flank steak and marinate in the refrigerator for 3 hours or more.

To make Peanut Sauce:
$1/4$ cup creamy peanut butter
$1/4$ cup water
2 tablespoons dried minced onions
1 or 2 teaspoons hot sauce
1 tablespoon cooking oil
1 teaspoon dried minced garlic chips
$1/2$ teaspoon salt
1 tablespoon lemon juice

Continued on next page

In a small frying pan add oil and fry onions and garlic until crisp. Remove and blot dry on paper towels. On low heat add peanut butter and half the water. Stir until well blended. Add hot sauce, lemon juice, sugar, salt, and remainder of the water. Blend and let cook for about 4 minutes. Remove from heat, let cool, then add onions and garlic. Remove to serving bowl.

Remove flank steak from refrigerator. Thread on thin wooden or bamboo skewers. Broil 3 minutes on each side. Serve with peanut sauce.

Chef's Tip: The skewers can be soaked in water to retard burning. The flank steak can be partly frozen to make slicing easier.

CHICKEN STIR FRY

Serves 2

This dish is low in fat and calories. Also, it is not expensive to make and the taste is wonderful because of the ingredients in the sauce.

1 chicken breast, skinned and boned
5 ounces fresh pea pods
1 small onion, quartered
5 fresh mushrooms, sliced
1 tablespoon soy sauce
1 teaspoon oyster sauce

1 teaspoon sesame oil
$^{1}/_{2}$ cup chicken broth
1 teaspoon cornstarch
3 tablespoons cashews
1 tablespoon cooking oil

Mix cornstarch with chicken broth until well blended. Add soy sauce, oyster sauce, sesame oil; set aside. Cut chicken breast into bite size pieces. In a wok on medium heat, add chicken and cook until all pink is gone. Add onions, pea pods and mushrooms; cook for about 4 minutes, tossing. Add broth sauce and cook until sauce thickens. Add cashews, toss and remove to heated serving bowl. Serve with cooked rice.

Chef's Tip: Chicken bones and skins are a wonderful source of fresh chicken stock; never discard them. In a large pot place bones and skin, just cover with water and boil for 15 minutes. Discard skin and bones. Strain stock. The stock will store in the refrigerator for 3 days or in the freezer for 3 months. When cold the fat can be skimmed off.

Variation: Cooking sherry can be substituted for soy sauce. This substitution will completely change the flavor of the sauce.

MACARONI AND CHEESE

Serves 4

Children love this dish and even like to make it. Be sure they are properly supervised concerning the boiling water and hot oven.

8 ounces macaroni, cooked and drained
1 - 8 ounce package of Velveeta® cheese
1 - 5 ounce can condensed milk
4 ounces ham, chopped
1 tablespoon pimentos
2 tablespoons onions, chopped
Salt and pepper to taste

Cook the macaroni in a large pot of boiling water. Stir frequently to prevent sticking to the pot. Drain well.

Chop the Velveeta® cheese into small squares. Add all ingredients and mix well. Bake in a 350° oven for about 45 - 50 minutes, or until the top is brown and bubbling.

Chef's Tip: The cheese and milk can be melted in the microwave.

SHRIMP AND PASTA

Serves 2

$^1/_4$ pound cooked shrimp
$1^1/_2$ cup butterfly pasta, cooked and drained
$^1/_4$ cup chili sauce
$^1/_2$ cup beef broth
$^1/_4$ cup onions, chopped
$^1/_4$ cup green pepper
1 tablespoon oil
$^1/_8$ teaspoon salt
$^1/_8$ teaspoon pepper
$^1/_8$ teaspoon garlic powder
$^1/_2$ cup Velveeta® cheese, cubed
$^3/_4$ cup mozzarella cheese, shredded

Saute the onions and green peppers in 1 tablespoon of oil until the onions are clear. Mix all ingredients thoroughly except the mozzarella cheese. Top with the mozzarella cheese and bake uncovered in a 350° oven for about 30 minutes.

GREEK LAMB BALLS IN CHERRY SAUCE

Serves 2

This recipe has a Middle Eastern flair because of the use of allspice and meat served with fruit.

Cherry Sauce:
$^1/_4$ cup dried cherries
4 tablespoons orange liqueur (soak cherries and liqueur overnight)
$^1/_2$ cup white cooking wine
1 teaspoon cornstarch, dissolved in
  2 tablespoons water

Lamb Balls
$^1/_2$ pound ground lamb (lean)
$^1/_8$ teaspoon allspice (ground)
Salt and pepper
1 egg yolk
4 tablespoons bread crumbs
2 tablespoons Parmesan cheese, ground or grated
1 teaspoon horseradish

Mix all lamb ingredients and shape into walnut size balls. Fry lamb balls over medium heat on all sides, and serve with sauce.

To make sauce, soak cherries in the liqueur overnight. Heat the wine and cherries over low heat. Add the cornstarch and water just before serving.

Chef's Tip: If you are making a large quantity of lamb balls and sauce, serve the lamb balls in the sauce. Dried cherries are expensive so I buy them at the bulk food counter in just the quantity that I need.

LEMON BAKED FISH

This is a low-calorie and low-fat dish.

1 large fish fillet (cod, walleye), about $1/2$ pound
4 thin slices onion
1 teaspoon lemon juice
Salt and pepper to taste

Brush the lemon juice on both sides of the fish. Salt and pepper to taste. Place fish on aluminum foil and place onion slices on top. Seal aluminum foil well and bake in 350° oven for 30 minutes.

Variations: Almost any type of salad dressing can be substituted for the lemon juice. Try french dressing or vinegar and oil.

THOM'S MULLIGAN STEW

Serves 4 to 6

This recipe was furnished by Ruth Hamilton, and she adds:
"Thom's Mulligan Stew is a recipe our son brought home from his
fifth grade cooking class. It's the only stew recipe I ever use."

1 $^1/_2$ pounds beef, cut up for stew
1 tablespoon shortening
Salt and pepper to taste
1 - 10 $^3/_4$ ounce can tomato soup
2 soup cans water
3 carrots, cut in 1-inch pieces
3 potatoes, cut up
2 onions, cut up small
$^1/_2$ cup celery, cut up
1 tablespoon green pepper, chopped

Brown the beef in the shortening. Remove to a large pot and add
the soup and water. Cook over low heat for 1 hour, covered.
When the meat is nearly tender, add the remaining ingredients and
cook over low heat for 30 minutes, or until the vegetables are
tender.

AUNT OLITH'S HAM LOAF

Serves 8

This recipe was furnished by Ruth Hamilton, and she adds: "Aunt Olith was my husband Dick's aunt but also my Home Ec teacher and a very dear friend. This was one of her recipes that our sons always looked forward to."

1 pound ground smoked ham
1 pound ground beef
2 cups corn flake crumbs
1 teaspoon ground cloves
2 eggs
$^1/_2$ teaspoon salt
1 cup milk

Combine all ingredients, mixing thoroughly. Divide and place in two loaf pans. Bake in a 350° oven about 45 minutes.

SOUTHERN CHICKEN AND DUMPLINGS

Serves 2

2 chicken thighs or 2 chicken breasts
3 tablespoons onions, chopped
4 tablespoons celery, chopped
1 tablespoon parsley
Salt and pepper to taste
1 cup Bisquick®
1/3 cup milk
2 tablespoons cornstarch
4 tablespoons cold water

In a 2-quart pan place chicken; just cover with water. Bring to a boil and reduce heat to a simmer for 15 minutes. Remove the chicken to cool. Strain the broth and clean the pot. Remove the skin from the chicken and discard. Cut the chicken from the bones and cut into bite size pieces. Place chicken, onions, celery, salt, pepper, and parsley in the broth and bring to a simmer.

Add milk to the Bisquick® and mix. Mix cornstarch into 4 tablespoons cold water and add to the broth. Stir until thickened.

Spoon dumplings (6) on top of the broth. Simmer uncovered for 10 minutes, then cover and simmer for another 10 minutes. Serve in the pot.

Chef's Tip: If you don't want to use a product like Bisquick®, make the biscuit recipe on page 77.

AMERICAN ROAST CHICKEN & DRESSING

Serves 4

1 roasting chicken (3 to 4 pounds)
1 - 8¹/₂ ounce box corn bread mix
1 - 14¹/₂ ounce can chicken broth
2 tablespoons onions, chopped
3 or 4 cooked sausage patties, optional
Salt and pepper to taste

Seasoned croutons
6 dried apricots
6 prunes
¹/₂ cup raisins
¹/₂ cup walnuts

Trim the fat from the chicken. Add the chicken neck and fat to a small pan of water and cook for 10 minutes. Discard fat and neck, strain the chicken broth. Make the corn bread Johnny cakes as directed on the package. Chop the fruit and walnuts rather fine.

In a large bowl layer the Johnny cakes, torn in bite size pieces, croutons (equal to amount of Johnny cakes), fruit, nuts, onions, salt, and pepper. Mix in chicken broth and mix well. *Note:* The dressing to stuff the chicken should be less moist because it will gain some of the moisture from the chicken. Stuff the chicken and skewer with bamboo skewers.

Add more chicken broth to the remainder of the dressing. Spoon the remainder of the dressing into a glass baking loaf pan.
Place the chicken on a wire rack in the broiling pan. Preheat the oven to 450°. Place the chicken in the oven and reduce the heat to 350°. The chicken should bake for 25 minutes per pound. The remainder of the dressing should bake for 45-50 minutes.

Chef's Tips: The pan dressing should be very moist. Use some of the homemade chicken broth as necessary. One can of chicken broth may not be enough.

STUFFED PORK CHOPS

Serves 2

2 thick cut pork chops, fat trimmed off
$1/4$ cup raisins
$1/4$ cup walnuts, chopped
3 dried apricot halves, finely chopped
$1/2$ cup seasoned croutons
$1/2$ cup chicken broth
2 tablespoons white cooking wine
Salt and pepper to taste

Cut a pocket in each pork chop, back to the bone. Brown pork chops on both sides in a hot frying pan. Set aside to cool. Mix remaining ingredients. Stuff dressing into each pork chop. Place pork chops in a glass loaf pan so that pockets are facing each other. Spoon remaining dressing over the cut sides. Add 2 tablespoons water in the bottom of the pan. Cover with aluminum foil and bake in a 350° oven for 1 hour 15 minutes.

Chef's Tip: Always purchase apricot halves from the bulk food counter. You can buy small amounts and the price is less. This goes for other ingredients such as walnuts and raisins.

COUNTRY FRIED STEAK

Serves 2

$^1/_2$ pound lean sirloin steak
$^1/_2$ cup flour
$^1/_2$ teaspoon salt
$^1/_2$ teaspoon seasoned pepper
$^1/_2$ teaspoon parsley flakes
$^1/_2$ teaspoon dry mustard
$^1/_2$ cup water
$^1/_2$ cup milk or 1 - $5^1/_2$ ounce can condensed milk
2 tablespoons cornstarch
$^1/_2$ teaspoon Kitchen Bouquet®

Cut steak into strips about 1-inch wide and 3 inches long. Mix flour, salt, pepper, mustard, and parsley. Dredge steak in flour and place on a cutting board. Beat the steak with the cutting side of a meat mallet, cross grain. The meat can be dipped several times in the flour. The idea is to beat the flour into the steak.

Mix water, cornstarch, and milk. Also add a small amount of salt and pepper. Add the Kitchen Bouquet® for color. Fry the steak on both sides until crisp, turning once. Remove to a hot serving dish. Add gravy mix to the frying pan and stir to loosen particles. When the gravy thickens it is ready to serve. The gravy can be served over the steak or separately. Serve with boiled or baked potatoes and a green vegetable.

Chef's Tip: When frying the steak and you notice the juice coming up to the top side, it's time to turn and fry the other side.

LAMB PATTIES AND CRANBERRY SAUCE

Serves 2

Most recipes take three or four tries before they are developed into a final product. This is one of the few that was made correctly the first time. Lamb served with nutmeg suggests that this dish could have been made in West Africa.

Cranberry Sauce:
1 cup cranberries, washed
1 apple, pared and finely chopped
1 orange, peeled and sectioned
1/4 cup sugar
3 tablespoons water or orange juice
1/4 cup walnuts, chopped
1/4 cup raisins
1/4 teaspoon cinnamon

Combine all ingredients except walnuts and simmer until the cranberries "pop" and almost all moisture is gone. Remove from heat and let cool. Refrigerate. Add walnuts just before serving.

Lamb Patties:
1/2 pound lean lamb sirloin, trimmed and ground
1 tablespoon white wine
1/4 teaspoon dill weed
1/4 ground nutmeg
Salt and seasoned pepper to taste
1 tablespoon cooking oil

Mix all ingredients well, divide into 4 patties. Place on waxed paper and mash into 4 patties. Store in the refrigerator for at least 2 hours. Heat oil in a frying pan and brown lamb patties well on both sides. Serve with either hot or cold cranberry sauce.

STIR-FRIED PORK AND VEGETABLES

Serves 2

1 lean center cut pork chop
1 cup pea pods
1 cup Chinese cabbage, shredded
1 small onion, quartered
1 tablespoon pimento
3 tablespoons salted peanuts (skins removed)
1 tablespoon cooking oil

Sauce:
¼ cup chicken broth, canned or fresh
1 tablespoon oyster sauce
Several drops of hot sauce
1 tablespoon soy sauce
1 teaspoon cornstarch

Mix all ingredients for the sauce and set aside. Trim the fat from the pork chop and cut into thin strips. In a wok add 1 tablespoon oil and heat to medium hot. Add the pork and fry, turning, until white. Add pea pods and onion, stir until almost tender. Add cabbage and pimento and continue to toss until cabbage starts to wilt. Add sauce, toss well and cook until sauce thickens. Remove to a heated serving dish. Add peanuts. Serve with hot cooked rice

CHICKEN ROLL-UPS

Serves 2

This recipe was entered in a contest. It didn't win a prize but the following month I saw it published in a magazine as advertising for spaghetti sauce.

1 - 14 ounce jar of spaghetti sauce
2 chicken breasts, skinned and boned
2 to 4 thin slices of ham
3 lasagna noodles, cooked and drained
1 cup cottage cheese
1 cup mozzarella cheese
1 small onion, sliced
Five-spice powder to taste
Salt and pepper to taste

Pound the chicken breasts until about ¼ inch thick. Place ham on chicken breast. Sprinkle with one large pinch of five-spice powder. Roll-up and skewer with a toothpick. Place in a loaf pan, to one side.

Spoon 3 large tablespoons of spaghetti sauce on the bottom of the other side of the loaf pan. Layer with one noodle, half of the cottage cheese, half of the mozzarella cheese, half the onion, salt and pepper, and several tablespoons of sauce. Repeat the process for a second layer and top with the remaining noodle. Spoon remaining sauce over the chicken and top of noodles. Cover with aluminum foil and bake for 1 hour 30 minutes at 350°.

BURGUNDY BEEF STEW

Serves 4

1 pound stew beef, cubed into 1-inch cubes
2 large potatoes, peeled and quartered
2 large onions, halved
1 cup carrots, sliced into 1-inch pieces
1 cup celery, sliced into 1-inch pieces
1 - 14^1/$_2$ ounce can beef broth
1 cup red cooking wine (Burgundy)
1 tablespoon fine herbs
3 tablespoons cornstarch
^{1}/$_4$ cup cold water
Salt and pepper to taste

In a large pot add beef, broth, and wine. Bake covered for 1 hour in a 350° oven. Add remaining ingredients and bake for 1 more hour or until vegetables are tender. Remove vegetables to a serving dish and place in the oven to keep warm.

Mix cornstarch and ^{1}/$_4$ cup cold water. Bring gravy to a boil on the stove top. Add cornstarch mixture, stir until gravy thickens. This dish can be served with the vegetables in the gravy, or with the gravy on the side. Serve with hot biscuits.

Note: This dish is perfect for a slow cooker. It takes about 5 hours and the step of baking the meat first is omitted. Vegetables cooked in a slow cooker remain more firm than convection cooking.

Chef's Tip: I always strain the broth before making gravy. This removes all the fine particles and makes the gravy smooth.

Comment: If the dish is served as leftovers, add 2 tablespoons water to the gravy when reheating. Also if the meat and vegetables are warmed in a microwave, add about 3 tablespoons beef broth and toss well before reheating.

BISCUITS & SAUSAGE GRAVY WITH CHIPPED BEEF

Serves 2

For a hardy breakfast or dinner, you just can't beat this combination. For breakfast serve with a side dish of fresh fruit; for dinner, a colorful salad goes well.

Biscuits (makes 6 biscuits):
1 cup self-rising flour
$1/2$ cup buttermilk, minus 2 tablespoons
$3^1/2$ ounces butter, room temperature
$1/8$ teaspoon salt

With a pastry cutter, blend very well the butter and salt into the flour. Mix in the buttermilk with a fork for 30 seconds. Roll out on a floured surface and knead for 30 seconds, no more. Pat into a circle $3/8$ inch high. Cut into biscuits with a 2-inch diameter glass. Place on a glass baking dish and bake in a preheated oven at 400° for 13 minutes.

Chef's Tips for Making Biscuits: There are two secrets in making biscuits. The first is you can work the butter into the flour as much as you wish before adding the buttermilk. As a matter of fact, the more the better. The second tip: after you add the buttermilk, mix for only 30 seconds and knead for only 30 seconds. The less you handle after adding the buttermilk, the lighter the biscuits will be. If the mixture is sticky, add a little flour, but not much.

Continued on next page

Sausage Gravy with Chipped Beef:
3 sausage patties
1 ounce chipped beef, torn into pieces
1 cup chicken broth
3 ounces condensed milk
$1/8$ teaspoon pepper
2 tablespoons onion, chopped
$1/2$ teaspoon parsley
Hot sauce (optional)
3 - 4 tablespoons Wondra® flour

Fry the sausage until crisp. Remove and chop quite fine. Remove all but 1 tablespoon of sausage fat. In the same pan, fry the onions until clear. Add the chicken broth and condensed milk, heat over low heat. Mix the flour in about 2 - 3 tablespoons of water and add to the gravy. Stir until it thickens. Add remaining ingredients and cook over low heat for about 7 minutes. Continue to stir. Serve over biscuits.

Chef's Tip: Mix 2 tablespoons of flour and 2 tablespoons of water in a small container. Do this twice. When adding the flour mixture to the gravy add a little at a time and let it cook for at least 3 minutes before adding more. When a new sack of flour is opened it is very dry. After it is opened it will absorb moisture. It is difficult to predict how much flour is needed to obtain the right thickness. This dish is also good as a leftover. Add 1 or 2 tablespoons of water before reheating.

CHINESE FRIED RICE

Serves 4

Fried rice is a favorite and is easy to make. The smoky links and green peas make this recipe very special.

3 cups cooked rice
1 - 10 ounce package smoky links
3 tablespoons onions, chopped
3 scallions, chopped with greens
$1/2$ of a 10 ounce package frozen green peas, thawed
1 egg
1 tablespoon hoisin sauce
1 tablespoon canola oil
1 tablespoon soy sauce

Cut smoky links in $1/4$ inch pieces. Beat the egg, fry 1 tablespoon at a time, remove from heat and slice lengthwise. Mix hoisin sauce and soy sauce, set aside.

Place oil in a wok and heat over medium heat. Add smoky links and cook until well browned. Add onions and scallions and cook for 1 minute. Add peas and cook 1 minute. Add rice and toss. Add hoisin sauce and toss. Serve with the egg slices on top.

Chef's Tip: The rice should be at room temperature. Cook and remove from heat, let stand until cool and break up with a fork. I use par boiled rice which doesn't stick together.

Variations: Almost any meat can be substituted for the smoky links. Try ham, chicken, pork, bacon, or shrimp, or any combination of these.

MICHIGAN GOULASH

Serves 4

This is an inexpensive dish that makes a colorful, hearty meal. Hot sauce can also be added to the sauce mixture for additional tang. Also, this is a dish that kids like to make (and eat).

1 pound lean ground beef
$^1/_4$ onion, diced
1 cup macaroni, cooked
Salt and pepper
1 cup sharp cheddar cheese, grated
$^1/_3$ cup ketchup
$^1/_3$ cup chili sauce
$^1/_3$ cup Picante sauce or V-8® juice

Brown ground beef, drain all fat off. Saute onions and add ground beef. Mix ketchup, chili sauce, and Picante sauce or V-8® juice. Salt and pepper to taste. Add macaroni and sauce, mix well. Cook for about 10 minutes on a low burner, then add cheese. Continue to cook until cheese is melted. Serve in the frying pan.

Serving Suggestion: Serve with a tossed salad.

STUFFED GREEN PEPPERS

Serves 2

1 large green pepper
1/4 pound lean ground beef
1/2 cup cooked rice
1/2 teaspoon garlic chips
3 tablespoons onions, chopped
1/3 cup ketchup
1/3 cup chili sauce
1/3 cup V-8® juice
1 tablespoon Picante sauce
Several drops hot sauce (optional)
1 teaspoon parsley
1 tablespoon salad mustard
1/2 teaspoon horseradish

Mix the ketchup, chili sauce, V-8® juice, Picante sauce, hot sauce, parsley, mustard, and horseradish; set aside. Cut the top off the green pepper and trim out seeds and pulp. Cut in half. Brown the ground beef and drain off all fat. Saute the onions.

In a medium bowl mix the beef, rice, garlic, onions, and half the sauce mixture. Spoon into the green peppers, place in a glass baking dish. Cover with remaining sauce. Cover tightly with aluminum foil. Bake in a preheated 350° oven for 1 hour and 15 minutes.

Chef's Tip: This dish serves well with baked sweet potatoes. They can be baked along with the green peppers.

JENSEN'S MEATBALLS

Serves 4 (about 20 - 24 meatballs)

*Meatballs are a standard bill-of-fare everywhere, but try this one.
It has taken almost 10 years of experimentation to perfect.*

1 pound lean ground beef
$^1/_2$ cup seasoned bread crumbs
1 medium onion, diced
1 large egg
1 teaspoon mustard
1 tablespoon parsley
$^1/_2$ teaspoon Worcestershire® sauce
2 tablespoons steak sauce
3 tablespoons Parmesan cheese, grated
2 tablespoons ketchup
Salt and pepper to taste
4 dashes hot sauce (optional)
1 teaspoon olive oil

In a large bowl, add all ingredients except the oil and mix
thoroughly. *Note:* When I make this dish I mix the ingredients by
squeezing with my hand. This may not be for you, but it is the best
way to blend the mixture and make firm meatballs.

Place a little oil in both hands and rub well. With a tablespoon,
dish out enough mixture to make a ball about 1 to 1$^1/_4$-inch and roll
into a ball shape. Place the balls on waxed paper. On low heat fry
the meatballs, turning often. The outside layer should be crisp.
These serve well with spaghetti. If meatballs are being made as an
appetizer they should not be over 1-inch in diameter. They can be
kept warm in a chafing dish of spaghetti sauce.

Continued on next page
82

In Tunisia stuffed meatballs are called Boulettes de Viande and are stuffed with potatoes and celery. After frying, they simmer in tomato sauce and red wine for about 30 minutes. Nutmeg is added to the sauce for flavor.

Stuffed Meatballs (Variation):
Stuffed meatballs are a delightful variation and a nice party treat. The same ingredients are used for the meatballs but when they are rolled into a ball, push your thumb into the center and make a deep depression. Next, insert one of the ingredients below and remold back into a ball.

Stuffings:
Stuffed green olives
Pitted black olives
Cocktail onions, pickled
Sweet or dill pickles (cut in olive size pieces)
Pickled beets (cut in olive size pieces)
Seedless grapes
Pineapple chunks

CITY CHICKEN

Serves 4 to 6

City Chicken is a very old Polish recipe. I first encountered it in Detroit about 1950. The Polish serve this dish at weddings and other special occasions. It is excellent as leftovers. As a matter of fact, when I make this dish I make extras just to have leftovers. City chicken is also good served cold.

1 1/4 pounds lean pork chops
1 pound veal steak, sirloin cut
1 large onion
1 egg
1 cup seasoned bread crumbs
Salt and pepper to taste
1 tablespoon parsley flakes
1 - 10 3/4 ounce can mushroom soup
12 skewers
2 tablespoons Parmesan cheese, grated
3 tablespoons olive oil
1 teaspoon Kitchen Bouquet®

Trim all fat from the veal and most of the fat from the pork. Cut into cubes about 1-inch square. Trim and slice the onion into thin slices. Beat the egg and set aside. Add the salt, pepper, parsley flakes, and Parmesan cheese to the bread crumbs and mix well.

Continued on the next page

CITY CHICKEN (CONTINUED)

Skewer pork and veal alternately on the skewer sticks. Each stick should have about 6 pieces of meat. Heat the oil in a frying pan over medium heat. Roll each city chicken in the egg and roll in the bread crumb mixture. Fry on all sides until brown. Remove to a large roasting pan.

Mix the mushroom soup with $1/3$ can of water and add the Kitchen Bouquet®. Add the sliced onions over the City Chicken and pour the soup mixture over the top. Cover and bake in a preheated oven at 350° for 1 hour 15 minutes.

Chef's Tip: Skewers can be obtained at most butcher markets or in the meat market of the grocery store.

Note: If you use a small roasting pan, you may have to add more soup mixture to cover the City Chicken. The soup mixture when cooked makes an excellent gravy for baked potatoes.

POLISH STUFFED CABBAGE

Serves 4 - 6

1 large head of cabbage
$^3/_4$ pound ground beef or ground pork
1 cup cooked rice
1 - $10^3/_4$ can tomato soup plus $^1/_2$ can water
$^1/_2$ cup Picante sauce
$^1/_2$ cup white cooking wine
1 small onion, chopped
$^1/_2$ teaspoon ground nutmeg
$^1/_8$ teaspoon garlic powder
5 tablespoons grated Parmesan cheese
Salt and pepper to taste

Cut the core out of the cabbage. Steam cabbage until outer leaves are limp. Remove outer leaves and continue the process until there are 12 to 14 leaves. The remainder of the cabbage can be used for another dish.

Saute the ground beef or pork until well cooked. Drain and place in a large mixing bowl. Saute onions until clear. Add onions, salt, pepper, rice, cheese, and ground nutmeg to mixing bowl and mix well. Trim the heavy spines from the cabbage leaves. Mix soup, wine, Picante sauce, and garlic powder.

In each cabbage leaf spoon 2 heaping tablespoons of meat mixture. Fold sides in and roll-up, secure the seam with a toothpick. Place seam side down in a large, heavy baking pan that has a lid. Continue the process until all leaves are used. If there is any meat leftover, place it on top of the cabbage rolls. Cover the cabbage rolls with the sauce mixture, cover and bake at 350° for 1 hour 30 minutes.

KRAUT AND CABBAGE

Serves 4

This recipe is a Polish dish that is easy to make and is a low-budget meal. If you substitute turkey sausage for the beef version it is also a low-calorie and low-fat dish. The Polish name is pronounced Ka-pu-sta.

1 - 15 ounce can sauerkraut
3 cups cabbage, chopped
1 small onion, chopped
7 ounces beef broth
Garlic powder
1 tablespoon dry mustard
Salt and pepper to taste
2 tablespoons parsley, chopped
2 tablespoons sugar
1 pound smoked Polish sausage

Rinse the sauerkraut under cold running water to remove the salty taste. Combine all ingredients and simmer for 45 to 50 minutes in a covered pot.

Chef's Tip: Fresh Polish sausage can be used in lieu of smoked sausage. Boil the fresh sausage until well cooked, then brown in a frying pan before adding to the sauerkraut and cabbage mixture. Also, this dish is better as a leftover.

CHICKEN AND GRAPES

Serves 2

This is a dish that takes 15 minutes to prepare and is a real treat. Almost any spreadable fruit can be used to change the flavor; try orange, cherry or blackberry.

1 whole chicken breast, boned (2 halves)
1 cup seasoned croutons
4 pitted dates
Chicken broth
Kitchen Bouquet® (optional)

Sauce:
$^1/_2$ cup grapes, cut in half
$^1/_2$ cup chicken broth
1 heaping tablespoon boysenberry spreadable fruit
1 teaspoon cornstarch mixed with 4 tablespoons cold water

Cut the dates into quarters. Mix croutons, dates, and chicken broth to soften. Place dressing in a glass loaf pan, making a mound in the center. Cover with the chicken breast. Paint with Kitchen Bouquet® for color (optional). Cover with aluminum foil. Bake in a 350° oven for 50 minutes.

About 10 minutes before the chicken is done, start the sauce. Heat the chicken broth to a light boil. Add cornstarch and water to thicken. Add grapes and boysenberry fruit and blend. Serve with sauce on the side. A colorful tossed salad goes well with this dish.

CHICKEN AND FRUIT

Serves 2

This delicate dish is low in calories, low in fat and very inexpensive. The taste is wonderful.

2 chicken breasts, skinned
3 tablespoons dried cherries
3 tablespoons dried pineapple, chopped
3 tablespoons raisins
3 tablespoons white wine
1 heaping tablespoon orange juice concentrate
1/4 cup water
1 teaspoon cornstarch

Soak the cherries, pineapple, and raisins in the white wine for at least 4 hours. While the chicken is broiling, combine the remaining ingredients and bring to a boil; reduce the heat to very low. When the chicken is well cooked on both sides, remove to a heated serving dish. Spoon the sauce over the chicken and serve. Garnish with fresh parsley.

JENSEN'S MEAT LOAF

Serves 4

$^1/_2$ pound lean ground beef
$^1/_2$ pound ground veal
Salt and pepper to taste
$^1/_4$ cup onions, chopped
1 teaspoon garlic chips or $^1/_2$ teaspoon garlic powder
2 tablespoons steak sauce
1 egg
$^1/_4$ cup seasoned bread crumbs
1 tablespoon salad mustard
$^1/_4$ cup ketchup

Preheat the oven to 350°. In a large bowl mix all ingredients
except the ketchup. Squeeze through your fingers to mix well.
Place in a glass loaf pan, spoon ketchup on top, and bake for 1 hour
15 minutes.

Chef's Tip: To add variety, stuff the meat loaf with stuffed olives.
Once the meat loaf is in the loaf pan, stick your thumb into it
several places and insert olives, then cover each hole. Another
variation is to add 1 or 2 hard boiled eggs into the center of the
meat loaf.

EASTERN LAMB STEW

Serves 4

1 pound lamb shoulder, trimmed and cubed
3 tablespoons cooking oil
1 - 15 ounce can tomatoes
$^1/_2$ cup onions, chopped
1 clove of garlic, diced
Salt and pepper to taste
1 cup white cooking wine
1 tablespoon cornstarch dissolved in 3 tablespoons water
1 teaspoon rosemary, crushed

Brown the lamb well on all sides in 3 tablespoons cooking oil.
Add the remaining ingredients and simmer for about 1 hour, or
until the lamb is tender. Serve over hot rice or noodles.

PORK CHOPS IN CHILI SAUCE

Serves 2

2 lean pork chops (center or loin cut)
$^1/_4$ cup white wine
3 tablespoons soy sauce
$^1/_4$ cup ketchup
$^1/_4$ cup chili sauce
1 tablespoon plus brown sugar
1 teaspoon dry mustard
Several drops of hot sauce

Marinate the pork chops in the wine and soy sauce for at least 4 hours or overnight. Blend the ketchup, chili sauce, brown sugar, and dry mustard; heat in the microwave for 20 seconds, or until the sugar is melted. Bake the pork chops covered with aluminum foil in a 350° oven for 1 hour. Remove and place sauce over the pork chops. Cover with aluminum foil and bake another half hour. Serve with a baked potato.

SALMON PATTIES

Serves 2

1 - 6 ounce can salmon
1 egg
$1/4$ cup seasoned bread crumbs
$1/8$ cup Parmesan cheese
$1/2$ teaspoon horseradish
4 drops hot sauce
$1/4$ teaspoon dill weed
Salt and pepper to taste
3 tablespoons cooking oil
2 tablespoons onions, chopped
3 tablespoons salsa
3 tablespoons ketchup or chili sauce

Mix all ingredients, except the salsa and ketchup, very well. Make 6 patties and place on waxed paper. Add 3 tablespoons of cooking oil to a frying pan; bring to medium heat.

Add salmon patties and fry until crisp. Turn over and fry the other side. Remove to a heated serving plate. Heat the salsa and ketchup in the microwave and spoon over the salmon patties or serve on the side.

SPICY STIR FRIED SHRIMP

$^1/_2$ pound raw shrimp, shelled and deveined
1 cup pea pods, trimmed and cut in half
1 cup celery, thinly sliced
$^1/_2$ cup onions, chopped
$^1/_2$ cup water chestnuts, sliced
2 tablespoons cooking oil

Sauce:
$^1/_2$ cup chicken broth
1 teaspoon oyster sauce
$^1/_2$ teaspoon sesame oil
$^1/_8$ teaspoon hot sauce
1 plus tablespoon cornstarch mixed with 3 tablespoons water

Mix all sauce ingredients and set aside. Add 2 tablespoons cooking oil to a hot wok. Stir fry the shrimp and celery until the shrimp turns pink (about 2 or 3 minutes). Add the onions, water chestnuts, and pea pods. Stir fry another 2 or 3 minutes. Add the sauce and toss to coat. Serve with hot cooked rice or chow mein noodles.

Chef's Tip: About rice: if possible, use parboiled rice. Parboiled rice separates much better than regular long grain rice.

OLD-FASHIONED LASAGNA

Serves 4 to 6

Meat Sauce:
1 pound ground beef
1 - 14 ounce jar of spaghetti sauce
Salt and pepper to taste
$^1/_2$ teaspoon cinnamon
$^1/_2$ teaspoon nutmeg
8 lasagna noodles, cooked
$^1/_2$ pound mozzarella cheese slices
$^1/_2$ pound ricotta cheese
1 onion, thinly sliced
$^1/_4$ cup grated Parmesan cheese

Cook the ground beef and drain well. Add the salt, pepper, cinnamon, nutmeg, and $^2/_3$ of the spaghetti sauce to the meat mixture. Grease the bottom of a $4^1/_2$ x 8-inch glass baking pan.

Layer the pan with noodles, meat sauce, mozzarella cheese, and onions. For the next layer, use ricotta cheese. Continue until all ingredients are layered. Top off with the remainder of spaghetti sauce and Parmesan cheese. Bake covered in a 350° oven for 45 minutes, uncover and bake an additional 15 minutes. Serve with a tossed salad.

Chef's Tip: For 2 servings, divide into two loaf pans and freeze one. Let thaw completely before baking. It's the cinnamon and nutmeg that make this dish special.

LONDON POT PIE

1 cup plus of leftover beef, chicken or ham, coarsely chopped
$^1/_2$ cup onions, chopped
1 cup plus potatoes, diced
1 cup carrots, diced
1 - 10$^3/_4$ ounce can mushroom soup
1 teaspoon Kitchen Bouquet®
5 ounces white wine
1 teaspoon parsley
Salt and pepper to taste
Prepared pie crust (top and bottom) - see recipe on page 163, or
    use commercial pie crust mix

Mix mushroom soup, Kitchen Bouquet®, wine, salt, pepper, and parsley very well. Mix all ingredients except the pie crust in a large mixing bowl. Line a pie pan with half the pie crust. Fold in the filling. Cover with the remaining pie crust after lining the lower edge with water. Flute with a fork and trim the edges with a knife. Bake in a 350° oven for 1 hour, or until well browned.

Chef's Tip: A small can of mushrooms can also be added. Drain well and pat dry with a paper towel.

SIMPLE BARBECUED BEEF

Serves 2

2 tablespoons onions, chopped
$^1/_2$ pound leftover roast beef
$^1/_2$ cup ketchup
1 tablespoon dry mustard
1 tablespoon vinegar
1 teaspoon sugar
1 teaspoon horseradish
2 tablespoons water
Salt and pepper to taste

Shred the beef. Mix all ingredients. Simmer on very low heat, stirring often. Cook for 15 minutes. Serve on toasted hamburger buns.

Chef's Tip: This dish can be made from canned beef. If canned beef is used, rinse the beef under cold water to remove the gravy. Canned beef works just as well as leftover beef and is less expensive. Also, leftover pork can be used in lieu of beef.

CORNISH HEN & WILD RICE

Serves 2

1 cornish hen, about 1 pound
$\frac{1}{2}$ cup cooked wild rice
$\frac{1}{2}$ cup apples, peeled and chopped
2 tablespoons orange juice
1 tablespoon onions, chopped
Salt and pepper to taste
2 tablespoons melted butter

Rub the melted butter on the outside of the cornish hen. Mix the stuffing ingredients and stuff the hen.

Bake on a rack in a 375° oven for 1 hour 15 minutes. If the hen is over 1 pound, bake an additional 15 minutes. Serve with a tossed salad.

CHINESE SWEET & SOUR PORK

Serves 2

Sauce:

$1/2$ cup water	Combine water and cornstarch.
$1/4$ cup white vinegar	Add all ingredients to a saucepan
$1/4$ cup sugar	and cook until sauce thickens.
$1/8$ cup chili sauce	Set aside and keep warm.
1 tablespoon cornstarch	

1 lean pork chop, 5-6 ounces trimmed and cubed in bite size pieces
$1/4$ cup sweet pickles, in bite size pieces
1 - 8 ounce can chunk pineapple, well drained
$1/2$ green pepper, in bite size pieces
$1/2$ ounce Chinese mushrooms
1 small onion, quartered
1 tablespoon cooking oil
5 or 6 maraschino cherries, cut in half

Soak mushrooms in warm water until tender. Squeeze dry and cut into bite size pieces. In a wok heat the oil over medium heat, add pork and cook on all sides until pink is gone. Add peppers and onions, stir fry until almost tender, about 2 minutes. Add remaining ingredients and stir fry until warm. Add sauce and toss well, cooking 1 more minute. Serve with cooked rice or chow mein noodles.

Variations: The sauce can be made with the drained pineapple juice substituted for water. If you do this cut the sugar in half. Other variations are to add 1 tablespoon sherry, or 1 tablespoon soy sauce.

99

CRAB CAKES WITH LEMON SAUCE

Serves 2

1 - 6 ounce can crab meat
1 tablespoon onions, chopped
$^1/_8$ teaspoon cayenne pepper
$^1/_4$ teaspoon salt
$^1/_8$ teaspoon pepper
1 egg, beaten
3 tablespoons flour
Bread crumbs

Drain crab meat well, press all the water. Mix all ingredients
except the bread crumbs. Make into patties about 2 inches in
diameter. Dust in bread crumbs and fry in 2 or 3 tablespoons oil on
both sides, until well browned.

Sauce:
2 tablespoons mayonnaise or salad dressing
2 tablespoons condensed milk
$^1/_2$ teaspoon salt
1 tablespoon lemon juice
$^1/_8$ teaspoon hot sauce

Mix all ingredients and serve with crab cakes.

STIR FRIED CHICKEN & BROCCOLI

Serves 2

1 half chicken breast, skinned, boned and cut into bite size pieces
1 cup broccoli flowerets, in bite size pieces
1 small onion, quartered
$^1/_2$ red pepper, in bite size pieces
1 garlic clove, chopped
3 tablespoons cooking oil

Sauce:
1 cup chicken broth
1 plus tablespoon cornstarch, mixed with
3 tablespoons water or broth
$^1/_8$ teaspoon hot sauce
1 tablespoon hoisin sauce
1 tablespoon cooking sherry
1 tablespoon soy sauce
Salt and pepper to taste

Mix all ingredients and set aside. Add 3 tablespoons cooking oil to a hot wok. Cook the chicken and garlic until the chicken is almost white. Add the remaining vegetables and stir fry for another 3 minutes. Add sauce and toss to coat. Serve with hot rice.

Chef's Tip: The chicken skin and bones can be cooked in water for the broth. If so, be sure to strain before using.

101

HAM AND SCALLOPED POTATOES

Serves 2

2 medium baking potatoes, thinly sliced
1 cup chicken broth
1 tablespoon parsley
3 ounces condensed milk
1 small onion, thinly sliced
6 ounces ham slices, cubed
2 teaspoons cornstarch mixed with
2 tablespoons water
Salt and pepper to taste
Butter

Slice the onion and potatoes thinly. Mix the cornstarch with 2 tablespoons water. Heat the chicken broth, salt, pepper, and parsley in a saucepan. Add the cornstarch to thicken. Add the condensed milk and set aside.

Layer a glass baking pan with layers of potatoes, onions, and ham. Dot with butter. Pour the broth mixture over the last layer of potatoes. Bake in a 350° oven for about 50 minutes, or until the potatoes are cooked.

Chef's Tip: The reason for thickening the broth on the stovetop first is to get the proper thickness.

Vegetables

NOTES

SPINACH AND BLUE CHEESE

Serves 2

5 ounces fresh or frozen chopped spinach
2 tablespoons onion, chopped
1 tablespoon sesame oil
1 teaspoon sesame seeds
1 tablespoon blue cheese
Salt and pepper to taste
2 tablespoons condensed milk

Cook the spinach in a little water for about 4 minutes. Drain and mash out all of the water. Add the sesame oil to a frying pan and cook the onions until clear. Add all remaining ingredients and cook for 3 or 4 minutes to warm.

105

STIR FRIED CABBAGE

Serves 2

2 large cups cabbage, shredded
1 small onion, sliced
¹/₂ cup chicken broth
Salt and pepper to taste
3 tablespoons white cooking wine
1 teaspoon parsley

In a frying pan, add chicken broth and bring to a full boil. Reduce heat to medium and add everything except the wine. Simmer covered about 10 minutes, or until the cabbage is cooked but firm. Add cooking wine, making sure all cabbage is covered. Remove to a serving bowl and sprinkle with paprika.

Chef's Tip: For a variation, grated Parmesan cheese can be added rather than paprika. Another variation is to add about ¹/₂ teaspoon horseradish to the chicken broth.

FRIED CABBAGE #2

Serves 2

2 cups cabbage, shredded
1 slice bacon
$^{1}/_{2}$ cup chicken broth
1 tablespoon seasoned vinegar
3 tablespoons white cooking wine
Salt and pepper to taste

Fry bacon until crisp, remove and crumble. Place cabbage in bacon drippings and toss to coat. On low heat add remaining ingredients. Saute until cabbage is tender. Sprinkle bacon over the top and serve.

Chef's Tip: If you have leftover cabbage from making stuffed cabbage rolls, this is a good use for it.

SESAME ASPARAGUS

Serves 2

$^1/_2$ pound fresh asparagus
1 tablespoon sesame oil
1 tablespoon sesame seeds

Cook the asparagus in boiling water and oil for about 3 or 4 minutes. Remove to a hot serving dish and sprinkle on the sesame seeds.

Chef's Tip: The purpose of adding the cooking oil to the water is to add a glaze to the asparagus so the sesame seeds will stick. Also, the water the asparagus is cooked in can be reused as a soup base.

WILTED LETTUCE

$^1/_4$ to $^1/_2$ head of lettuce
1 slice of bacon, fried and crumbled
Salt and seasoned pepper
1 tablespoon vinegar

Tear (don't cut) bite size pieces of the lettuce in a bowl. Heat bacon drippings until quite hot. Add salt and pepper to the lettuce. Add lettuce to the hot oil and toss until covered, not more than 5 or 6 seconds. Remove from heat and place in a serving dish. Sprinkle bacon over the lettuce.

Chef's Tip: If you don't like the texture of wilted lettuce, you can make a hot bacon dressing. Use 1 tablespoon bacon drippings, 2 tablespoons vinegar, 1 teaspoon sugar and heat in a microwave to dissolve the sugar. Add dressing to the lettuce, toss well to coat, and sprinkle bacon over the top.

FRIED CARROTS

Serves 2

2 large carrots
2 tablespoons white cooking wine
2 tablespoons brown sugar
1 tablespoon butter

Peel and slice the carrots. Place in boiling water and cook until almost tender. Drain and set aside. Melt the butter in a frying pan. Add the cooking wine and carrots. Drizzle the brown sugar over the carrots and let it melt.

Variation: Honey can be used in lieu of brown sugar.

BROILED TOMATOES

Serves 2

2 large tomatoes
$1/8$ cup onions, chopped
3 tablespoons dry seasoned bread crumbs
2 large mushrooms, finely chopped
2 tablespoons grated Parmesan cheese
Salt and pepper to taste
2 tablespoons cooking sherry

Cut the tops off the tomatoes and discard. Spoon out the insides of the tomatoes and chop finely. Saute the chopped tomatoes, onions, mushrooms, bread crumbs, salt, and pepper for about 3 minutes. Spoon back into the tomatoes and top with cheese. Broil until the cheese melts.

DAD'S SAUERKRAUT

Makes about 9 gallons

There is nothing like homemade sauerkraut. This recipe is from Maurice Ogden, my Father-in-law, who enjoyed gardening and growing his own cabbage for sauerkraut. The original recipe dates back to the turn of the century.

40 pounds cabbage shredded (save outer cabbage leaves)
$^3/_4$ to 1 pound kosher salt

Shred one head cabbage, sprinkle with salt and pound with sauerkraut pounder (or use a half-gallon jug or pop bottle).

Continue layers until finished. Use outer cabbage leaves over top. Weigh down with a large plate, stone or jug. Cover with clean cloth or towel. Leave in cool spot (inside at about 60 to 70 degrees) for approximately 10 days.

Check frequently. If mold appears in juice, skim it off. Keep checking and tasting until it suits your taste. Put in containers or bags and refrigerate or freeze.

Note: You can make a smaller quantity if you aren't up to shredding 40 pounds of cabbage!

Chef's Tip: Here's a favorite Ogden recipe for Sauerkraut Casserole: 1 cup ham, baked or boiled, 3 cups sauerkraut, $1^1/_2$ tablespoons lemon juice, 2 medium apples, sliced. Cut ham in $^1/_2$-inch pieces; mix ham, lemon juice and sauerkraut in casserole. Place a layer of kraut mixture on the bottom, then a layer of sliced apples until all is used. A few slices of apple with peeling left on is pretty on top. Cover and bake for 30 minutes at 350°.

CHARD, SPINACH, OR BEET GREENS

Serves 2

About 5 or 6 ounces of chard, spinach, or beet greens
$^1/_2$ lemon and 2 lemon slices
Salt
Seasoned pepper

Wash and trim the greens. In a large pot of salted, boiling water (about $^1/_4$ inch), boil the greens for 3 or 4 minutes. Don't overcook.

Drain greens well and squeeze the lemon half over the top. Remove to a hot serving dish and garnish with lemon slices and seasoned pepper.

Chef's Tip: Seasoned vinegar can be used for a variation.

GERMAN STYLE RED CABBAGE

Serves 4

Red cabbage is a standard bill of fare in most German restaurants.

$1/2$ head red cabbage, core removed and thinly sliced
1 tart apple, peeled and finely sliced
$1/4$ cup vinegar
$1/8$ cup sugar
Salt and pepper to taste
$1/4$ cup red wine
1 garlic clove, finely sliced
1 small onion, thinly sliced

Cook all ingredients in a covered pan on low heat for about 30 minutes. Stir occasionally.

Chef's Tip: This dish serves well with pork roast. Also this is a good leftover dish that can be warmed in the microwave.

OVEN FRIED POTATOES

Serves 2

2 large baking potatoes
Nonfat cooking spray

Peel the potatoes. Slice into uniform french fry strips. Spray a cookie sheet with the nonfat cooking spray. Place potatoes on the cookie sheet. Spray with nonfat cooking spray. Bake in a 375° oven for about 40 minutes, turning once.

Chef's Tip: The baking time will vary depending on the crispiness desired. Also, if you slice the potatoes into irregular slices, some will be more crisp than other.

Serving Suggestion: Sprinkle with salt, pepper, and McCormick® salad seasoning. If you wish to omit the nonfat cooking spray, place about 1 tablespoon of cooking oil in the palm of your hand and rub the potatoes all over. Doing this it is not necessary to oil the cookie sheet.

ROASTED CORN

Roasting corn this way gives it a wonderful flavor.

Ears of corn in the husk
Salted cold water
Butter, melted

Soak the corn in the salted water for 4 hours. Roast outdoors on a low fire grill for about 1 hour, turning every 15 minutes. Pull back the husk (use as a handle) and paint with butter.

Chef's Tip: <u>The corn is very hot so be sure to use kitchen gloves when pulling back the husk</u>. If you have a shelf on your grill, place the corn on the shelf and use the grill to cook something else. With a shelf the heat can be turned up.

TWICE-BAKED POTATOES #1

Serves 2

2 baking potatoes
2 tablespoons mayonnaise
2 tablespoons onion, chopped
2 tablespoons strong cheese; i.e., blue cheese,
   roquefort, Stilton, or Cheshire
1 tablespoon bread crumbs
1 tablespoon Parmesan cheese, grated
Salt and pepper to taste

Bake the potatoes until soft, about 50 to 60 minutes in a 350°
oven. Remove and cut in half. Spoon out the inside to a mixing
bowl. Mash in the mayonnaise, onion, and strong cheese. Add
salt and pepper. Spoon back into the shells and dust with
Parmesan cheese and bread crumbs. Place under the broiler until
the tops are brown.

Chef's Tip: This dish also works well when something is being
broiled. You can place the potatoes on a lower shelf to keep warm,
then transfer them to the broiling shelf just before serving.

117

TWICE-BAKED POTATOES #2

Serves 2

2 baking potatoes
1 tablespoon onions, chopped
1 teaspoon bacon bits
3 tablespoons cheddar cheese, grated
Salt and pepper to taste

In a 350° oven, bake the potatoes until tender. Remove potatoes, cut in half and scoop out almost to the skin. Add remaining ingredients and mash potatoes. Fill skins with mashed potatoes and broil until the tops are crisp.

MARY'S BRUSSELS SPROUTS

Serves Mary

My wife, Mary, is a brussels sprout freak, so I created this recipe for her. I don't even like brussels sprouts, but this dish is good!

$1/2$ pound brussels sprouts, trimmed and cleaned
3 tablespoons butter
$1/2$ teaspoon Hungarian paprika
$1/4$ teaspoon curry powder
$1/2$ teaspoon sharp mustard (dijon style)
Salt and pepper to taste

Boil brussels sprouts until tender, drain well. Cut the sprouts in half. In a frying pan add butter, melt over low heat, and add remaining ingredients, mix well. Add sprouts, cut side down. Cook over low heat until sprouts are well warmed. Remove to a heated serving dish.

STIR FRIED PEA PODS

Serves 2

$^1/_4$ pound pea pods
$^1/_4$ pound bean sprouts, fresh
1 teaspoon seasoned vinegar
1 tablespoon rice wine
2 tablespoons cooking oil
1 small onion, chopped
Salt and pepper to taste

Heat the oil in a wok or frying pan. Add pea pods, onion, and bean sprouts, then saute for about 2 minutes. Add vinegar and rice wine, toss to coat. Remove to a hot serving dish.

Chef's Tip: This is an excellent way to use leftover bean sprouts from an Egg Fu Yung dish.

ACORN SQUASH

Serves 2

1 small acorn squash
1/8 cup raisins
2 teaspoons brown sugar (or 2 tablespoons honey)
2 teaspoons butter

Cut the squash in half and spoon out seeds and stringy material. Place raisins, brown sugar, and butter in each half. Cover tightly with aluminum foil and bake in a 350° oven for 1 hour, or until squash is tender.

121

FRIED SWEET POTATOES

Serves 2

If you are a sweet potato fan, this recipe is for you!

1 cooked sweet potato (leftover)
1 tablespoon brown sugar
1 tablespoon butter
$^1/_2$ cup marshmallows

Peel the sweet potato and slice approximately $^3/_4$ inch thick. Melt the butter in a frying pan. Heat the sweet potato slices until warmed through. Timing is the key here! Add the brown sugar on top of the sweet potato slices. Turn each slice over to caramelize. Add the marshmallows. After the marshmallows have melted, slide the sweet potatoes to a serving dish, so that the marshmallows are up.

CREAMED SPINACH

Serves 4

This is a wonderful dish to serve with roast pork.
Even if you don't like spinach, you will love this creation.

1 - 10 ounce package frozen spinach, chopped
1 - 3 ounce package cream cheese, chive type
2 tablespoons seasoned rice vinegar
1 tablespoon white cooking wine
$1/8$ teaspoon basil leaves
$1/8$ teaspoon tarragon leaves
Salt and pepper to taste

Cook the spinach as directed on the package. Drain and mash out most of the water. Heat the cream cheese in the microwave for 10 seconds to soften. In a glass baking dish, mix all ingredients very well. Bake for 30 minutes in a 350° oven, uncovered.

Chef's Tip: If you can't find the chive type cream cheese, add $1/2$ teaspoon dried chives or 1 teaspoon chopped fresh chives.

NUTMEG SPINACH

Serves 4

1 - 10 ounce package fresh or frozen spinach, chopped
2 tablespoons onions, chopped
1 tablespoon cooking oil (olive oil or canola)
$1/4$ teaspoon nutmeg
Salt and seasoned pepper to taste
5 tablespoons condensed milk or cream
1 tablespoon cooking sherry

Cook spinach as directed, then drain well. Saute onions in oil until clear but not brown. Add spinach, salt, pepper, and nutmeg and heat thoroughly. Add milk or cream; heat thoroughly again. Add sherry and toss.

DEPRESSION POTATOES

During the Great Depression many families used beans and potatoes as their main staple, as my family did. Clever cooks looked for ways to change the taste of potatoes and different ways to serve them. This variation was developed by my Mother. It's a real treat.

2 medium to large cooking potatoes
2 heaping tablespoons mayonnaise
3 tablespoons onions, chopped
Salt and white pepper to taste

Peel and slice potatoes. Boil in water until tender. Drain water well. Keep the potatoes in the pot to keep hot. Mash well. Add remaining ingredients and whip. Serve immediately.

Chef's Tip: After the potatoes are drained, place the pot back on the hot burner for about a minute. Be sure to shake the pot or stir the potatoes with a spoon or fork. This will reduce the remaining moisture to steam and dry the potatoes.

SOUTHERN GREEN BEANS

Serves 4

This is a Southern dish. The beans are "cooked down" until they are very soft. When I make this dish, my wife, Mary, says, "Oh, boy, oh, boy, green beans!"

1 pound fresh green beans, ends snipped and cut into 1-inch pieces
4 slices bacon, fried (reserve 2 tablespoons drippings)
1 cup chicken broth
4 tablespoons onions, chopped
Salt and pepper
1 teaspoon fine herbs

Fry bacon until crisp. Crumble and add to chicken broth. Add 2 tablespoons bacon drippings to chicken broth. Add remaining ingredients, bring to a boil. Reduce heat and simmer, covered, for 35 minutes or more.

BAKED BEANS

Serves 4 plus

2 - 15 ounce cans of beans in tomato sauce
1 tablespoon dried onions
1 tablespoon molasses
2 tablespoons brown sugar
$^1/_2$ cup ketchup or chili sauce
1 tablespoon salad mustard
$^1/_2$ teaspoon garlic powder
1 or 2 tablespoons salsa or Picante sauce

Open the cans and spoon off all the tomato sauce on the top. Mix all ingredients well in a large bowl. Bake 1 hour 30 minutes in a 350° oven.

Chef's Tip: When you see beans in tomato sauce on sale, buy four to six cans. The less expensive beans make the best baked beans. You can make this dish for about 75 cents and if you purchase one of the better brands of beans it will cost that much for half the quantity.

FRIED CAULIFLOWER

Serves 4

This is an old Polish recipe served at weddings. The cauliflower should be quite firm after being boiled. The frying makes it tender and delicious.

$^1/_2$ large head cauliflower, trimmed and cut into flowerets
1 cup seasoned bread crumbs
$^1/_4$ cup Parmesan cheese, grated
Salt and pepper to taste
4 tablespoons canola oil
2 eggs, beaten

Boil the cauliflower in a large pot until almost tender. Drain well. Mix bread crumbs, cheese, salt, and pepper in a low dish. Dip cauliflower in egg mixture, roll in bread crumb mixture, and fry on all sides until golden brown.

NUTTY ZUCCHINI

Serves 2

1 medium zucchini
1 small onion, sliced
2 tablespoons canola oil
2 tablespoons white cooking wine
Salt and pepper to taste
3 tablespoons walnuts

Slice the zucchini into ¼ inch slices. Add canola oil to a frying pan, add onions, and cook until almost done, but firm. Add zucchini and cook both sides until almost done. Salt and pepper to taste, then add cooking wine and make sure all slices are covered. Add walnuts.

Chef's Tip: To leach out some of the water from the zucchini, place on paper towels and sprinkle with salt (both sides). Let zucchini stand for 15 minutes, rinse, and pat dry with paper towels.

CUCUMBERS IN SOUR CREAM

Serves 2

Cucumbers in Sour Cream is a wonderful Greek dish.

1 cucumber, peeled and thinly sliced
Salt and pepper to taste
1 tablespoon fresh or dried mint leaves
1 cup sour cream
Garlic powder to taste

Mix all ingredients well and marinate in the refrigerator for 3 hours before serving.

Chef's Tip: You can use $^1/_2$ cup of sour cream and $^1/_2$ cup of yogurt for a nice change.

CUCUMBERS IN WINE AND VINEGAR

Serves 2

1 cucumber, peeled and thinly sliced
4 tablespoons seasoned rice vinegar
4 tablespoons white cooking wine
$1/8$ teaspoon garlic powder
Salt and pepper to taste

Mix all ingredients well and marinate in the refrigerator for 3 hours before serving.

Chef's Tip: Marinating the cucumbers will make them wilted. If you like firm cucumbers, marinate only for 30 minutes.

MARINATED BRUSSELS SPROUTS

Serves 4

1 pound brussels sprouts
2 tablespoons cooking oil
4 tablespoons tarragon vinegar
1 teaspoon dill weed
1 tablespoon lemon juice
1 teaspoon dried chives
Salt and pepper to taste

Parboil the brussels sprouts, leaving them very firm. Drain and cut into halves. Mix all ingredients and place in the refrigerator overnight to marinate.

Before serving, bring to room temperature.

STIR FRIED ASPARAGUS

Serves 2

¹/₂ pound fresh asparagus
2 tablespoons cooking oil
1 teaspoon sesame oil
1 teaspoon sesame seeds
3 slices of medium onion
2 tablespoons red pimento

Trim off the asparagus stalks. Cut asparagus into bite size pieces. Heat cooking oil and sesame oil in a wok or heavy frying pan. Add the asparagus, onion, sesame seeds, and pimento. Stir fry until the asparagus turns bright green. Lightly add the salt and pepper. Remove to a heated serving dish.

CHEESY POTATOES

4 medium to large potatoes
1 - 10³/₄ ounce can cream of celery soup
1 - 10 ounce package smoky links
1¹/₂ cups sharp cheese, grated
1 teaspoon minced dried onions
1 teaspoon parsley
¹/₂ soup can of water
¹/₂ soup can of condensed milk
Salt and pepper to taste

Slice the smoky links, crosswise, in ¹/₄ inch slices. Mix the soup, water, milk, onions, parsley, salt, and pepper very well. You may have to microwave for a minute or two to get the soup, water, and milk to blend well.

Peel and slice the potatoes thinly. In a covered glass baking dish, layer potatoes, cheese, and smoky links until the potatoes, cheese, and smoky links are used. Top with sauce mixture. Bake in a 350° oven for 40 minutes, uncover and continue baking for another 20 minutes, or until the potatoes are done.

Sauces

NOTES

THE WONDER SAUCE

Try this one! You have to taste it to see that it really is the Wonder Sauce.

2 tablespoons blackberry jam
1/2 cup chicken stock or broth
1/8 teaspoon cinnamon
1 tablespoon lemon juice
1/2 teaspoon cornstarch, plus 1 tablespoon water

Mix the cornstarch and water. Mix all other ingredients and heat. Add cornstarch to thicken.

Chef's Tip: Try the Wonder Sauce over ice cream or frozen yogurt. Add raisins for another change of taste.

Serving Suggestion: This sauce can be served over chicken, ham, pork, or lamb patties.

PIZZA SAUCE

Open a can or jar of sauce for your next pizza? Not this time. Try this pizza sauce and get the kids involved in making it.

3 ounces tomato paste
3 ounces beer
2 tablespoons Picante sauce
$1/2$ teaspoon dry mustard
$1/8$ teaspoon garlic powder
1 teaspoon brown sugar
1 tablespoon vinegar
1 tablespoon Worcestershire® sauce
Salt and pepper to taste
Several drops of hot sauce, optional

Combine all ingredients, heat over low heat to blend.

Chef's Tip: Double the recipe for spaghetti sauce and add 1 teaspoon of fine herbs. If it is too thick add 1 or 2 tablespoons of beer.

ROQUEFORT OR BLUE CHEESE DRESSING

Makes about 1¹/₂ cups

1 - 3 ounce package Roquefort or Blue cheese
¹/₂ cup mayonnaise
¹/₂ cup sour cream
¹/₂ teaspoon horseradish
1 teaspoon lemon juice
Salt to taste

Crumble cheese in a bowl. Add remaining ingredients and mix well.

Chef's Tip: This dish will keep well in the refrigerator for about 3 days. In addition to salads, it can be served over baked potatoes, or use as a dip.

SHRIMP SAUCE #1

Serves 2

Both of these shrimp sauces can be used for shrimp or fish. Each has a distinctive flavor.

2 tablespoons chili sauce
2 tablespoons ketchup
1 teaspoon horseradish
A few drops of hot sauce

Mix all ingredients.

SHRIMP SAUCE #2

2 tablespoons ketchup
2 tablespoons Picante sauce
1 teaspoon horseradish
1 teaspoon lemon juice

Mix all ingredients.

140

VINEGAR DRESSING #1

Makes about ¹/₄ cup each

1 tablespoon olive oil
3 tablespoons seasoned rice vinegar (Nakano® brand)
3 tablespoons red cooking wine
¹/₄ teaspoon sugar
¹/₄ teaspoon salt
¹/₄ teaspoon seasoned pepper (McCormick® brand)

Mix all ingredients and warm in a microwave to melt the sugar and salt.

VINEGAR DRESSING #2

1 tablespoon olive oil
3 tablespoons raspberry wine vinegar (Reese® brand)
3 tablespoons white cooking wine
¹/₄ teaspoon sugar
¹/₄ teaspoon salt
¹/₄ teaspoon seasoned pepper (McCormick® brand)

Mix all ingredients and warm in microwave to melt the sugar and salt.

Chef's Tip: It's not often that I mention brand name products, but to make these Vinegar Dressings taste right the products shown above are a must.

DRESSING FOR FISH

One serving

1 tablespoon dijon mustard
1 tablespoon lemon juice
1 tablespoon honey

Mix all ingredients well. Microwave for 20 seconds. Mix well.
Serve over broiled or baked fish.

Variation: Broiling fish can dry it out. Try this variation. Place a
single serving of white fish on aluminum foil. Dot with butter.
Place several thin slices of onion over the fish and top with the fish
dressing above. Bake in a 350° oven for 20 minutes.

PLUM SAUCE

Jane Alexander, a very dear family friend, furnished this recipe in memory of her special Grandmother-in-law, Madeline Michelini. Madeline was an avid gardener and cook, with over 400 cookbooks in her personal collection.

1 clove garlic, peeled
1¹/₂ tablespoons plum jam
2 tablespoons white vinegar
1 tablespoon sugar
1 tablespoon dry mustard

Rub the sides of a small serving dish with the peeled garlic. Combine the jam, vinegar, and sugar in the serving dish. Place the dry mustard in another small dish. Add drops of water gradually to the mustard and stir vigorously until a smooth paste develops. Spoon the mustard gently into the center of the plum sauce. <u>Don't stir.</u> This sauce is especially good with egg rolls, but also goes well with lamb, pork or ham.

Chef's Tip: Jane advises that the longer you stir the dry mustard with drops of water, the hotter it gets!

BONA COTA (THE GOOD SAUCE)

Jane Alexander, a very dear family friend, furnished this recipe in memory of her special Grandmother-in-law, Madeline Michelini. Madeline always made her own Italian bread to go with the vegetables and Bona Cota sauce.

Sauce:
1 stick of butter
$1/2$ cup olive oil
2 cloves of garlic
1 or 2 cans of flat anchovies

Vegetables for dipping:
Cucumber
Carrots
Celery
Green onions
Green or red pepper

Leaf lettuce (fancy Italian, not iceberg)
Zucchini (fresh)
Tomato
Crusty Italian bread

Melt the butter slowly in a pan. Add the olive oil. Use a garlic press and add the garlic. Heat mixture until it bubbles. Add anchovies and let simmer. Stir until anchovies have almost dissolved. Place mixture in a heating dish.

Slice vegetables into long strips. The vegetables are to be dipped in the sauce and served with the crusty Italian bread. Also serve with red wine.

Chef's Tip: Jane tells me that you must eat this sauce while hot, and the crusty Italian bread is a must!

144

Desserts

NOTES

MOLASSES SNAPS

Makes 4 dozen

2^{1}/$_{4}$ cups flour
1 teaspoon soda
1 teaspoon cinnamon
^{1}/$_{2}$ teaspoon nutmeg
1 teaspoon allspice
^{1}/$_{2}$ teaspoon ground cloves
1 cup brown sugar, firmly packed
^{3}/$_{4}$ cup shortening
^{1}/$_{4}$ cup molasses
1 large egg
White sugar for topping
^{1}/$_{8}$ teaspoon salt

Mix flour, soda, cinnamon, nutmeg, allspice, and salt. Set aside. Beat the shortening and brown sugar until well blended; add egg and molasses. Stir in flour mixture and chill for 1 hour. Shape cookies into balls about an inch in diameter and roll in white sugar. Place the balls on an ungreased cookie sheet about 3 inches apart. Bake in a 350° oven for 10 - 12 minutes, or until the tops have cracked.

APPLE-PINEAPPLE CRISP

Serves 6 - 8

4 cups apples, peeled and sliced
1 cup pineapple chunks, drained
1 cup white sugar
1 teaspoon cinnamon
$^{1}/_{8}$ teaspoon nutmeg
$^{1}/_{8}$ teaspoon ginger
1 cup rolled oats
$^{1}/_{2}$ cup flour
$^{1}/_{2}$ cup butter, melted
$^{1}/_{2}$ cup walnuts, chopped
$^{1}/_{2}$ cup brown sugar

Line the bottom and sides of a pie pan with 1 teaspoon melted butter. Mix the apples, white sugar, cinnamon, nutmeg, and ginger. Drain the pineapple well and pat dry with paper towels. Add to the apple mixture.

Mix the oats, flour, brown sugar, melted butter, and walnuts very well. Place the apples in the pie pan. Top with the oats. Bake for 45 minutes in a 350° oven.

Chef's Tip: Use tart apples. If sweet apples are used, reduce the white sugar. When topping the apples with the oats use 2 tablespoons to assist in spreading the mixture evenly.

FRIED BANANAS

If you like bananas you will love my recipe for Fried Bananas. This is another original from Chef Dinosaur.

1 large banana (firm)
$1/8$ cup dried cherries
$1/8$ teaspoon cinnamon
1 teaspoon brown sugar
3 tablespoons orange liqueur
1 tablespoon butter

Soak the cherries in the orange liqueur overnight. Peel and slice the banana in half, then slice lengthwise. Melt the butter in a frying pan; add the banana slices and heat. Add the cherries and orange liqueur mixture. Sprinkle the cinnamon over the bananas. Sprinkle the brown sugar over the cherries. Heat through and divide in two serving dishes.

Chef's Tip: You may want to substitute pears in this recipe. It's wonderful too. Also, try it with ice cream.

PAULINE'S AWARD WINNING APPLE PIE

This is my Mother-in-law, Pauline Ogden's, Apple Pie, and it's the best I have ever eaten.

Crust:
2½ cups flour
½ teaspoon salt
1 cup shortening
1 tablespoon sugar
1 egg beaten with ⅓ cup cold water
1 tablespoon vinegar

Cut flour, salt, shortening, and sugar until very fine crumbs. Add egg, water, and vinegar to flour mixture. Add more water by tablespoons until it sticks together and you are able to handle.

Apple Filling:
6 cooking apples, peeled and sliced
1 cup white sugar (less is apples are sweet)
1 teaspoon cinnamon
Dash of salt
2 tablespoons brown sugar
Dots of butter over the top of the apples

Roll out crust and line bottom of pie pan. Toss apples, white sugar, cinnamon, and salt in a bowl. Place in pie pan. Sprinkle with brown sugar and dots of butter. Place top crust over pie; trim and press edges with fingers. Make design with tip of knife to allow steam to escape. Bake at 350° for about 55 minutes, or until crust is golden and juice is thickened.

150

GRANDMA VIRGINIA'S PEANUT BUTTER COOKIES

Makes about 40 cookies

This recipe was furnished by Ruth Hamilton. In her note to me she adds: "Grandma Virginia is my Mother and not only was I raised on these good peanut butter cookies, but our sons, and now our grandchildren enjoy them."

1 cup white sugar
1 cup brown sugar
1 cup peanut butter
$1/2$ teaspoon salt
2 eggs
$2/3$ cup shortening
1 teaspoon vanilla
2 cups flour
2 teaspoons baking soda

Sift the flour and baking soda together. Cream the sugar, shortening, eggs, and peanut butter. Add flour, salt, and vanilla. Roll the dough and place the cookies on an ungreased cookie sheet. Each cookie should be about the size of a hickory nut. Bake for about 10 minutes in a 325° oven.

ANGEL WINGS BY AUNT JANE

Makes about 30

This is an old Polish recipe that is light and tasty. I know how to pronounce the name in Polish, but I don't know how to spell it in English. You can say it this way: crew-sheek-ees.

9 egg yolks, beaten well
1¹/₂ tablespoons sugar
2 tablespoons melted butter
³/₄ teaspoon vanilla
1 teaspoon lemon juice
1 tablespoon bourbon or whiskey (optional)
Flour

Combine all ingredients with enough flour to make the dough stiff enough to roll out. Cover and let stand at least 2 hours or longer. Roll out on wax paper until dough is about ¹/₈ inch thick. Cut in diamond shapes (2 inches wide by 4 inches long). Fry in deep fat fryer until brown. Remove and drain on paper toweling. Sprinkle with powdered sugar. Serve as a cookie.

MARY'S PUMPKIN FRUITCAKE

1 loaf cake

Mary, my wife, and I even made pumpkin soup once, just once! Just ask Michelle and Greg DeWitt.

1³/₄ cups flour
1 teaspoon baking powder
1 teaspoon baking soda
1 teaspoon cinnamon
¹/₂ teaspoon ground cloves
1 teaspoon salt
1 cup sugar
¹/₂ cup shortening
1 egg, beaten
1¹/₂ cup canned or fresh pumpkin
¹/₂ cup raisins
¹/₂ cup mixed candied fruit
1 cup walnuts, chopped

Sift together the flour, baking powder, baking soda, cinnamon, cloves, salt, and sugar. Combine the egg and pumpkin and mix well. Use a little of the flour mixture to dredge the fruit. Add flour mixture to pumpkin in thirds. Fold in fruit and nuts. Bake in a loaf pan or tube tin for 1 hour 15 minutes at 325°.

BREAKFAST COOKIES

Makes about 36 - 48

This recipe was furnished by our friend, Marcheta Haile, and in her words: "These cookies really get you moving!" Marcheta was named by her Dad after the song, Marcheta (A Love Song of Old Mexico) by Victor Schertzinger.

$^1/_2$ cup melted margarine
$1^1/_3$ cup light brown sugar
3 eggs
3 apples, chopped with skins
2 cups whole wheat flour
$^1/_2$ cup white flour
1 cup oat or wheat bran
$^1/_2$ cup wheat germ
1 cup plus oatmeal
1 teaspoon soda
1 teaspoon baking powder
1 cup nuts, chopped
1 teaspoon cinnamon
$^1/_2$ teaspoon nutmeg
1 cup golden or dark raisins or dates

Blend eggs and apples in a blender. Combine dry ingredients and mix well with apple mixture. Add fruit and nuts. Drop by tablespoon on a cookie sheet and bake for 12 - 15 minutes in a 350° oven.

OATMEAL ICEBOX COOKIES

Makes about 36

This recipe was furnished by Pauline Ogden, my Mother-in-law. These cookies are a family favorite among the Ogdens.

1 cup shortening
1 cup brown sugar
1 cup white sugar
3 cups quick oatmeal
1 1/2 cups flour
1 teaspoon soda
1/2 teaspoon salt
1 teaspoon vanilla
2 eggs

Mix all ingredients with hands. Roll in wax paper and set in the refrigerator overnight. Slice and bake at 350° for 10 to 15 minutes.

LEMON COCONUT COOKIES

Makes 3 dozen

This recipe was furnished by a dear friend, JoAnn Harris. She said the recipe was given to her by a friend, who also received it from a friend. No wonder it became a favorite!

$^3/_4$ cup butter (room temperature)
$^1/_2$ cup sugar
1 egg
1 teaspoon vanilla
$^1/_2$ teaspoon lemon extract
2 cups sifted flour
$1^1/_3$ cups flaked coconut

Cream butter and sugar until light and fluffy. Beat in egg, vanilla, and lemon extract. Blend in flour and coconut. Shape in walnut size balls. Place on greased baking sheet, flatten with fork. Bake in moderate oven (350°) about 8 to 10 minutes, or until edges are lightly browned. When cool, frost with Lemon Butter Frosting.

Lemon Butter Frosting:
$^1/_4$ cup butter (room temperature)
1 teaspoon grated lemon peel
$^1/_8$ teaspoon salt
2 cups sifted powdered sugar
3 to 4 teaspoons lemon juice

Mix butter, lemon peel, salt, and powdered sugar. Add lemon juice, sparingly to start, until frosting is the right consistency to frost cookies. *Note:* A half batch of frosting will frost about $^3/_4$ of the cookies with a thin layer.

156

BLUEBERRY CRISP

Makes 8 x 8 pan

This recipe was furnished by Arlene Poel. The Poels own a blueberry plantation in Spring Lake, Michigan. Her blueberry recipes are always delicious!

1 cup flour
1 cup brown sugar
$^3/_4$ cup oatmeal
$^1/_4$ teaspoon cinnamon
$^1/_4$ teaspoon salt

Mix all ingredients and pat half of the mixture in an 8 x 8-inch pan.

Add:
2 cups fresh blueberries

Cook together:
1 cup white sugar
2 tablespoons cornstarch
1 cup water
1 teaspoon lemon juice
$^1/_2$ cup blueberries

Pour cooked mixture over fresh blueberries. Pat rest of the topping over the blueberry mixture. Bake at 350° for 45 minutes. Serve with ice cream, yogurt, or whipped cream.

PUMPKIN-CHOCOLATE CHIP COOKIES

Makes 4 dozen

My daughter, Susan Nicks (Nicki), furnished this recipe. She has created some wonderful recipes, and this is just one!

1 cup honey
$^1/_2$ cup butter or margarine
1 egg
$3^1/_4$ cups whole wheat pastry flour
$1^1/_4$ teaspoons soda
$1^1/_4$ teaspoons baking powder
$^1/_2$ teaspoon salt
$1^1/_2$ cups mashed pumpkin
1 teaspoon vanilla
1 cup chocolate chips or carob chips
1 cup chopped nuts

Cream sugar and butter, add egg and mix well. Sift dry ingredients, add alternately with pumpkin to wet ingredients. Stir in vanilla, nuts, and chips. Place cookies on greased baking sheet. Bake 10 to 12 minutes in a 350° oven.

MIRIAM'S CHEESECAKE

1 9-inch cheesecake

This cheesecake recipe was furnished by Miriam Cross, a very nice lady and a wonderful cook. You will love her cheesecake recipe, as everyone does!

Graham cracker crumbs
1 pound small curd cream style cottage cheese (dry version)
2 - 8 ounce packages cream cheese, softened
1½ cups sugar
4 eggs, slightly beaten
⅓ cup cornstarch
2 tablespoons lemon juice
½ cup margarine, melted
1 pint sour cream
1 teaspoon vanilla

Grease 1 - 9-inch spring-form pan; dust with graham cracker crumbs.

Mash cottage cheese through a large strainer into a large mixing bowl. Add cream cheese and beat at high speed until well blended and creamy. At high speed, blend in sugar, then eggs. At low speed, add cornstarch, lemon juice, and vanilla. Beat until blended. Add melted margarine and sour cream; blend on low speed. Pour into prepared pan.

Bake at 325° about 1 hour 10 minutes, or until firm around the edges. Turn off oven; leave cheesecake in oven for 2 hours. Cool on wire rack. Chill, then remove side. This recipe also freezes well.

159

HOLIDAY FRUIT CAKE

Makes one loaf

1 cup golden raisins
1 cup dates, chopped
1 cup cherries, candied
1 cup pineapple, candied
1 cup pecans
1 cup walnuts
4 eggs
$^3/_4$ cup flour
$^3/_4$ cup sugar
$^1/_2$ teaspoon nutmeg
$^1/_2$ teaspoon cinnamon
$1^1/_3$ cup graham crackers, crushed
$^1/_2$ teaspoon baking powder
$^1/_2$ teaspoon salt

Beat the eggs in a large bowl. Mix the remaining ingredients very well. Grease the bottom and sides of a glass loaf pan with margarine or nonfat spray. Place the cake mixture in the loaf pan, pressing out all the air.

Bake in a 350° oven for about 40 to 45 minutes, or until a skewer comes out clean. Remove from oven and let cool. Remove from the pan.

Optional: Soak a large cheesecloth in 1 cup of apricot brandy. Wrap the chessecloth around the cake, cover with aluminum foil for a day.

Other

NOTES

FOOLPROOF PIE CRUST

Makes two 9-inch double crusts, plus one 9-inch shell

This recipe was furnished by Pauline Ogden, my Mother-in-law. I have eaten her apple pies for over 20 years; they are so good they could win an award! Her recipe for apple pie is on page 150 in the dessert section.

5 cups flour
2 cups vegetable shortening
1 tablespoon sugar
2 teaspoons salt
1 tablespoon vinegar
1 egg
$^1/_2$ cup water

With a fork mix together the flour, shortening, sugar, and salt. In a separate dish, beat the vinegar, egg, and water. Combine the two mixtures, stirring with a fork until all ingredients are moistened, then with hands mold dough in a ball. <u>Chill at least 15 minutes</u> before rolling it into desired shape.

Dough can be left in refrigerator up to 3 days, or it can be frozen until ready to use.

Chef's Tip: Dough will remain soft in the refrigerator and can be taken out and rolled at once.

163

DEPRESSION SPREAD

Serves 4

Several comments about Depression Spread: I know the ingredients sound weird, but you will have to try this one to believe it! It is delicious. This recipe was developed during the depression when dessert was out of the question for many families. It is great for parties, but let your guests try some before you tell them what is in it.

$^1/_3$ cup mayonnaise
$^1/_3$ cup ketchup
$^1/_3$ cup peanut butter
2 dashes hot sauce, optional

Blend all ingredients until smooth. Serve with crackers, or use as a dip for vegetables.

CANNED PEPPERS

Makes 2 pint jars

Homemade canned peppers are a treat. They are not only better than store bought, but less expensive. This is an old Polish recipe that was developed at the turn of the century by a very nice Polish lady who lived in Detroit. In the early 1950s, I used to take her mushroom hunting in the woods. I was in my early twenties and she was in her late fifties, but I couldn't keep up with her. Her name was Katherine Sionkowski.

1 pound Hungarian peppers
1 Jalapeno pepper (half for each jar)
1 cup white vinegar
1 cup water
$^1/_4$ cup sugar
$^1/_4$ cup honey
1 teaspoon pickling spices
1 teaspoon salt
1 garlic clove, diced

Cut the stems from the peppers. Cut in half and remove the seeds and pulp. Blanch the peppers in boiling water until tender and crisp, but not soft. Remove the peppers to cold water. Add remaining ingredients and cook to melt the sugar and honey. Remove from heat and let cool.

Stuff the jars with the peppers. Add the vinegar and water mixture to cover the peppers. Store in the refrigerator for one week. After a week in the refrigerator they are ready to eat. They will keep in the refrigerator about three weeks.

Chef's Tip: After one week, I remove the Jalapeno pepper half from each jar. This makes a tangy pepper but not too hot. **Warning:** After handling the Jalapeno pepper, be sure to wash your hands with soap and water.

165

PICKLED CAULIFLOWER

Makes 2 pints

1 small head cauliflower
1 hot pepper (half for each jar)
1 cup white vinegar
$^1/_4$ cup sugar
$^1/_4$ cup honey
1 teaspoon pickling spice
1 teaspoon salt
1 garlic clove, chopped
1 cup water

Cut the flowerets into bite size pieces. Blanch in boiling water, with the hot pepper, until just tender and crisp. Remove and drain.

Add all remaining ingredients and bring to a boil. Remove from heat and let cool. Stuff the cauliflower into 2 pint jars that have been sterilized. Fill with pickling juice. Store in the refrigerator for one week.

Chef's Tip: The hot pepper can be removed after a week if you don't like the cauliflower too hot.

APPLESAUCE

Makes 2 pints

10 cooking apples, peeled, cored, and sliced
Sugar or brown sugar
Cinnamon
Ground cloves
Ground ginger

In a very small amount of water or orange juice, cook the apples over low heat until they are reduced to sauce. Season to taste with the sugar, cinnamon, cloves, and ginger.

Chef's Tip: Apples that work well for applesauce are Golden Delicious, McIntosh, or the older variety of Duchess. Also, the amount of sugar used will depend on the apple tartness. After the applesauce cooks it can be stored in plastic containers and will keep well in the freezer.

STUFFED EGGS

Serves 4

4 large eggs
2 tablespoons mayonnaise
1 teaspoon sweet relish
4 olives (cut in half)
$^1/_2$ teaspoon mustard
$^1/_2$ teaspoon horseradish
1 teaspoon Parmesan cheese (grated)
Salt
Pepper
Paprika

Hard boil the eggs, let cool and peel. Slice the eggs in half, lengthways, and remove the yolks to a side bowl. Add all ingredients except the olives and blend until smooth. Spoon yolk mixture into the egg whites and top with olives. Chill before serving. Dust with paprika.

Chef's Tip: Eggs will accept many types of seasonings. Several variations are listed below.

For Moisture:
French dressing
Sour cream
Sweet pickle juice

For Stuffing:
Anchovies
Liver pate
Cream cheese
Smoked salmon
Deviled ham

168

CORN BREAD DRESSING

Serves 8

When I was a boy my Mother made this Corn Bread Dressing almost every Sunday. She used a fat stewing hen to produce the chicken broth. Today I use canned chicken broth to reduce the fat content and to lower the calorie count.

1 - 8½ ounce package corn muffin mix
Seasoned croutons
Salt and pepper
½ cup chopped onions
½ cup chopped celery
Chicken broth, canned or stock (about 14 to 20 ounces)
4 or 5 fried sausage patties, cut into small pieces (optional)

As directed on the corn muffin mix, make Johnny cakes. Preheat oven to 350°. In a large bowl tear 2 or 3 Johnny cakes into bite size pieces. Add an equal amount of croutons. Add celery, onions, sausage, salt, and pepper. Repeat the process until all Johnny cakes are used.

Wet down with chicken broth and mix with a spoon. It is difficult to tell just how much chicken broth is required because some croutons absorb more or less juice. The mixture should be very wet but not sloppy. Transfer to a loaf pan and bake about 1 hour 15 minutes. To test, a probe should come out almost clean. The edges should be crisp.

Chef's Tip: This is an old southern style dressing and it is wonderful. The dressing can be stuffed into a turkey or part of it into a roasting chicken with the balance baked in a loaf pan. If baked in a turkey or chicken, the mixture should use less chicken broth because it will absorb some of the turkey or chicken juice. Also, this is a fine leftover dish. Eat it cold or pan fry in butter until crisp. By the way, the richer the chicken broth, the better it is! ***You have to try this one - it's a winner.***

169

CHICKEN WINGS

Serves 6

12 chicken wings
1 cup white wine
1 cup flour
Salt and pepper
$^{1}/_{2}$ cup sesame seeds
1 tablespoon ginger
1 tablespoon hot sauce

Cut wing tips off and discard. Cut remaining wings into 2 pieces. Wash and pat dry with paper towels. Mix wine and hot sauce, add wings, and marinate in the refrigerator for three hours.

Mix flour, salt, pepper, ginger, and sesame seeds well. Shake off excess wine and roll wings in flour mixture. Place on a baking pan and bake at 350° for one hour. Serve hot.

Chef's Tip: Sesame seeds are expensive but can be purchased at most stores as bulk food. You won't believe the cost savings. This is an inexpensive finger food for a large crowd.

BOILED COFFEE

About 4 cups

If you like coffee, you have to try this one. This is how coffee was made for years outdoors and before there were coffee pots as we know them today. The egg shell is added to remove any bitter taste from the coffee.

5 cups cold water
5 tablespoons coffee
1 egg shell

Add all ingredients to a large pot and bring to a boil. Reduce heat and simmer 5 minutes. Remove from the heat and let grounds settle. Ladle into coffee cups or mugs.

171

FRIED BEAN SANDWICH

Serves 4

This is a takeoff of my Dad's recipe. He liked to fry beans and add hot sauce. Most of the time there was as much hot sauce as beans!

1 - 16 ounce can pinto beans, well drained (reserve liquid)
4 thick slices onion (about 2-inch diameter)
1 cup sharp cheddar cheese, grated
4 slices bread, toasted
4 large tablespoons salsa sauce
Salt and pepper to taste
4 tablespoons white wine
Hot sauce to taste (optional)

Mash the beans (add some reserved bean liquid if the beans are too dry), then add wine. Fry the beans until well heated, turning often. Spoon the beans on the toast. Add onion and top with cheese. Broil until cheese is melted and bubbling. Remove, add salsa, garnish with fresh parsley and serve.

Chef's Tip: Several drops of hot sauce can be added to the beans before mashing. Beans can be mashed using a potato masher. If the beans are dry, add 2 or 3 tablespoons of the reserved liquid from the beans.

172

HARVEST PANCAKE

Serves 4

This delicious recipe was furnished by my daughter, Nicki. She comments: "It tastes better the more you eat!"

Filling:
¹/₄ cup butter
3 cups sliced apples
¹/₃ cup maple syrup
¹/₄ cup apple cider, juice or water
1¹/₄ teaspoons cinnamon

Pancake:
4 eggs
¹/₄ teaspoon salt
²/₃ cup flour
¹/₃ cup milk
¹/₄ cup maple syrup
2 tablespoons butter

1 tablespoon oil or butter for skillet

Filling:
Melt butter, add apples, maple syrup, cider, and cinnamon. Cook over low heat for about 3 to 5 minutes. Remove from heat.

Pancake:
Beat eggs until fluffy enough to make soft mounds. Alternately beat in flour/salt and milk/maple syrup. Add 2 tablespoons melted butter and beat until just smooth.

Preheat oven to 425°. Put 1 tablespoon oil or butter in 10-inch ovenproof skillet, pour batter into skillet. Bake 5 minutes. Remove and spoon filling over the top. Return to oven, reduce heat to 375°. Bake for 12 minutes. Serve hot.

FRUIT PIZZA

Makes 1 - 12-inch pizza

This Fruit Pizza was furnished by Mary Vivian, a close, long-time friend. It makes a colorful, tasty pizza that will bring compliments from your guests.

Crust:
$^1/_2$ cup margarine
$^1/_4$ cup white sugar
$^1/_4$ cup brown sugar
1 cup flour
$^1/_2$ teaspoon baking soda
$^1/_2$ teaspoon cream of tartar
$^1/_4$ teaspoon salt

Mix margarine, white sugar, and brown sugar well, then add flour, baking soda, cream of tartar, and salt. Press dough on pizza pan. Bake 10 to 15 minutes at 350°, or until just lightly browned. Cool.

Spread with:
8 ounces cream cheese, or plain yogurt, well drained
$^1/_3$ cup sugar

Top with fruit of your choice:
Bananas, kiwi, grapes, strawberries, peaches, nectarines, etc.

Glaze (optional): Cook until thick, cool. Pour over fruit.
$^1/_2$ cup sugar
$^1/_8$ teaspoon salt
2 tablespoons cornstarch
$^1/_2$ cup orange juice
$^1/_2$ cup water

NEVER FAIL NOODLES

Serves 2

This is another old Polish recipe. The first time I made this recipe I made a huge quantity and had noodles drying all over the house.

2 egg yolks
1 teaspoon shortening
2 tablespoons cream
$1/4$ teaspoon baking powder
$2/3$ cup sifted flour

Blend egg yolks, shortening, cream, salt, and baking powder. Add the flour and mix well. Roll out on a floured board to $1/16$ inch thick and cut into thin strips. Remove to waxed paper and allow to dry for at least five hours. To cook, boil in salted water as you would any packaged noodles.

LIVER PATE

Serves 4 to 6

This is an old Jewish recipe. If you make it the Jewish way, you must use Kosher salt.

1 pound chicken livers
2 tablespoons onions, finely chopped
1 hard boiled egg
4 tablespoons chicken broth (or more)
2 tablespoons cooking sherry
Salt and pepper to taste

Cut the chicken livers in half and trim off all fat. Discard any livers that are discolored. Boil the chicken livers in water for about 10 minutes. Mash the chicken livers with a fork until they are very fine or process in a food processor. Add the remaining ingredients and mix well. Dish into a serving bowl and chill.

Chef's Tip: The amount of chicken broth you add will vary from batch to batch. Serve with crackers or on party rye bread.

SWEET WON TONS

This is a very popular party finger food.

1 - 12 ounce can apricot filling
1 package Won Ton skins

Divide the apricot filling into four bowls.

Filling #1 - Add:
1 teaspoon brown sugar
1 tablespoon sesame seeds
3 tablespoons chopped walnuts

Filling #2 - Add:
3 tablespoons chopped raisins soaked in a flavored
    liqueur such as orange, cherry, peach, etc.
1 tablespoon brown sugar

Filling #3 - Add:
1 teaspoon brown sugar
3 tablespoons chopped dates

Filling #4 - Add:
3 tablespoons peanut butter

Continued on next page

Mix all four fillings well. Place 1 teaspoon of filling in the center of a Won Ton skin. Moisten two edges with water. Fold to make a triangle. Press out as much air as possible. Moisten the edges of the triangle and fold the edges to make a diamond shape. Continue until all filling is used. Deep fry in 375 - 400° oil for 4 or 5 minutes, or until golden brown. Remove to paper toweling. Serve hot.

Chef's Tip: Won Tons can be reheated in a 350° oven for 5 to 7 minutes. Also Won Tons can be frozen. Thaw at room temperature and reheat in the oven as above.

Almost any combination of filling can be used (apricot, cherry or date). Also, try a crushed Clark® bar or Baby Ruth® candy bar. They are wonderful.

SHOESTRING OMELETTE

Serves 2

3 eggs
1 cup frozen shoestring potatoes
¼ cup onions, chopped
¼ cup sharp cheese, grated
5 slices bacon
Salt and pepper to taste
¼ cup Picante sauce (room temperature)

Fry the bacon until crisp, remove and drain on paper towels.
Remove all but 2 tablespoons of bacon grease. Fry the potatoes
(adding the onions about halfway through the frying process) until
golden brown and crisp. Remove and set aside.

Beat the eggs with the salt and pepper. In a medium hot frying pan
cook the eggs, tipping the pan while lifting the edges. When the
bottom is cooked and the top is almost cooked, place the potatoes,
onions, and bacon on one-half of the omelette. Turn the other half
over the potatoes. Sprinkle on the cheese and Picante sauce.
When the cheese is melted, remove to a warm platter.

SALSA SCRAMBLED EGGS

Serves 2

3 or 4 eggs
¹/₄ cup onions, chopped
Salt and seasoned pepper
¹/₄ cup salsa

Beat the eggs with the salt and pepper. Cook the onions in a small amount of oil until clear. Turn the heat up to high and scramble the eggs very fast. Remove to a hot serving dish and top with salsa.

Chef's Tip: Scrambled eggs are best when cooked very rapidly. I like them a bit on the runny side, others prefer them more firm. Another cooking tip is to add half an egg shell of water to the egg mixture. This adds steam and will reduce the cooking time.

SNAILS (ESCARGOT)

Serves 6

For a dinner party serve this dish as an appetizer. You will win rave reviews!

1 - 4¹/₂ ounce can giant snails (12 to a can)
¹/₄ cup onions, finely chopped
¹/₄ cup mushrooms, finely chopped
1 package frozen pastry shells, puff type
Salt and pepper to taste
Garlic powder
Butter

Bake the pastry shells according to the directions on the package. Drain the snails and rinse under cold water, drain well. Saute the snails, onions, mushrooms, garlic powder, salt, and pepper in butter for about 3 minutes. Fill the pastry shells and serve.

BAGEL CHIPS

4 Bagels

This recipe sure beats what you can buy at the store.

4 bagels
McCormick Salad Supreme® seasoning
Salt
Garlic powder
Butter

Slice the bagels into thin slices, as thin as possible. Melt the butter and use a pastry brush to dot one side of the bagel chips. Sprinkle with salad seasoning, salt, and garlic powder. Bake in a 200° oven for about 45 plus minutes, or until crisp.

Chef's Tip: The bagels will slice better if they are cut into quarters. Also, baking time will vary depending on the amount of moisture in the bagel. Try other ingredients such as hot pepper, salt, and garlic chips. I have cooked chips for an hour or more to get the desired crispness.

FRENCH TOAST

It's the vanilla and cooking sherry that make this dish special.

4 slices white bread
2 eggs
$1/2$ teaspoon vanilla
1 tablespoon cooking sherry
2 tablespoons cooking oil
Maple syrup

Beat the eggs, vanilla, and sherry. Dip the bread in the egg mixture and fry on both sides. Serve with the maple syrup.

Chef's Tip: Try using a variety of breads such as cinnamon, raisin, or apple. Also, I butter both sides of the bread before frying, but this is optional.

MEATBALLS AND CHERRIES

Makes about 32

This is a fine appetizer that serves well at a party or any special occasion.

Sauce:
1 - 21 ounce can of cherry pie filling
6 ounces chili sauce
6 ounces ketchup
$1/4$ cup brown sugar
2 tablespoons lemon juice
$1/2$ teaspoon hot sauce

Mix all ingredients and heat well to melt the sugar.

Meatballs:
$1 1/4$ pound lean ground beef
$1/2$ cup seasoned bread crumbs
2 tablespoons dried onions
1 tablespoon Worcestershire® sauce
1 egg
3 tablespoons parsley
$1/2$ teaspoon garlic powder
Salt and pepper to taste

Mix all ingredients very well and shape into 1-inch balls. Place meatballs in a 9 x 13 x 2-inch glass baking pan. Cover with the cherry sauce and bake in a 350° oven for about 35 minutes. Serve in the baking dish.

Chef's Tip: Leftovers, if there are any, can be warmed in the microwave.

184

Herbs, Oils & Tips

NOTES

ABOUT COOKING OILS

It is very difficult to cook some dishes without using a little cooking oil. I use three kinds of cooking oil: canola oil, corn oil, and olive oil. Canola oil has the least amount of saturated fat, while olive oil has the most, twice as much.

When I use olive oil it is for dishes that require a higher heat and I use it very sparingly.

Margarine has about the same amount of saturated fat as olive oil. Cooking with butter makes everything taste better but at a price. Butter has seven times the amount of saturated fat as canola oil.

It is generally accepted that polyunsaturated fat will lower one's blood cholesterol when substituted for saturated fats. Regular corn oil has twice as much polyunsaturated fat as canola oil.

The best overall choice is corn oil for cooking. The ones to stay away from are beef tallow (lard), butter, and coconut oil. As an example, coconut oil has 12 times the amount of saturated fat as canola oil.

MEAL PLANNING AND SHOPPING

It is very important to plan the week's cooking before a shopping trip. I generally do this around a Saturday and Sunday cooking schedule. Everyone likes good food but never has the time to spend in the kitchen. More time is usually available on the weekend for cooking.

There are many weeks when I cook large meals on both Saturday and Sunday to provide leftovers for quick meals during the week. Some dishes are better than others for leftovers. These include most soups, such as bean soup, chili, corn chowder, and chicken soup. There are others that don't keep as well. These include cream of asparagus, spinach soup, and French onion.

Some of the best main dishes that work well as leftovers are city chicken, stew, beef roast, stuffed cabbage, and meatballs. On the other hand some dishes are not candidates for leftovers. These include all stir-fry dishes, flank steak, and stuffed green peppers.

Some main dishes freeze well and consideration should be given to preparing more than one main dish with the second to be frozen for a quick oven meal. These include lasagna, stuffed pork chops, and chicken rollups. There are some foods that don't keep well at all and should be used no longer than a day or two after purchase. These include chicken livers and all forms of fish.

If you shop at a supermarket it is very important to shop on the same day the market puts out fresh fish. Pay close attention to the packing and selling dates that are on the package. Here are several rules to follow for sell dates.

1. Fish should have at least 5 days
2. Chicken livers, at least 5 days
3. Chicken and pork, at least 7 days
4. Beef, 5 to 7 days
5. Milk, at least a week
6. Orange and grapefruit juice, 10 days
7. Cheese, up to 2 weeks (fresh packed)

Buying at the bulk food counter can reduce the food bill considerably. Items such as spices, dried fruit, dates, nuts, and pasta are much less expensive when purchased in bulk.

Don't overlook the major discount stores, such as K-Mart® and Wal-Mart®, as a place to reduce your shopping bill. Items such as canned fruit juice, canned salmon, ketchup, and even canned pork and beans can be purchased at good savings.

It is my belief that everyone who cooks should write a cookbook. The key is to experiment. After you have mastered some of the simple cooking skills, start to invent your own recipes. Discover what spices work well with different meats. Cooking main dishes with fresh and dried fruit can provide an exciting, different meal.

One last important tip: keep notes in your cookbooks. On the cover sheet of a new cookbook, write down the recipe name and page number of ones to try. Also, on the recipe page, jot down any changes, additions, or deletions. This will improve your performance the next time around.

TIPS ON MAKING SOUP

A good pot of soup is something like an art form to me. There are many rules you should follow in making good soup. Listed below are some rules I have developed over the years in my soup kitchen.

UTENSILS

If you are going to make good soup you must start with the right utensils. I always use a stainless steel four-quart pot. An enamel one will do just as well but never use an aluminum pot. Aluminum pots have their place in the kitchen, I suppose, but not for cooking.

COOKING TIME

Good soup should never be hurried. Cook it on a low burner and simmer it; never boil it. When adding vegetables that have different cooking time, like potatoes and onions, try and back schedule, adding the vegetables that take the longest first and those with the least cooking time last. This way all of the vegetables will have the same degree of firmness.

STRAINING STOCK

As you review the soup recipes in Chapter 1, you will note each time I boil meat to get it tender I either discard the stock (for some soups) or strain it and wash the pot. I think soup will taste much better if the pot is cleaned before cooking vegetables. It is an extra step but worth the effort.

CHICKEN BONES

I must have over 100 cookbooks in my library. As a matter of fact, I read cookbooks like others read novels. I have one cookbook that has a chicken stir-fry recipe in it and part of the instructions read: "trim the chicken breast and discard the bones." Not in my kitchen!

There are many recipes that call for chicken stock. Place the chicken bones in a large pot just covered with water. Boil for 10 to 15 minutes, then discard the bones and skin, strain, and store in the refrigerator for up to one week, or freeze. Don't let that good stock go to waste.

ADDING SPICES AND WINE

Spices should be added as early in the cooking process as possible and wine should be added at the last minute. Soup pots should be covered at all times and stirred every 10 minutes or so. Taste testing should be made near the end of the cooking process and any corrections made then.

All soups, except creamed ones, should rest for an hour, then be reheated before serving.

LEFTOVERS

Leftover meats and vegetables can be added to soups and recooked. This sometimes adds an interesting flavor.

THICKENING

Basically there are several ways to thicken soup. In the bean soup recipe, for example, I add extra beans. After they are cooked, I remove some and run them through a blender. This method works well for bean and potato soup.

Potatoes can be cooked separately, blended and added to vegetable soup, but I think this changes the flavor of the soup too much. Flour can be used to thicken soup, but in my opinion this adds a starchy taste.

Cornstarch or powdered tapioca also work well. For cornstarch I use about two tablespoons mixed with about four table-spoons of cold water, to blend. Add this mixture to the soup and stir in for about three or four minutes while the soup is very hot. Take care not to add additional cornstarch before the first batch has had a chance to thicken.

It is also important to add cornstarch to hot, but not boiling, soup. If the soup is too hot when adding the cornstarch, it will glob up. This is also true when adding cornstarch to a sauce.

HOW TO SAVE SOUP

I made a batch of yellow split pea soup one time and in experimenting, I added too much sherry. At the tasting process, the sherry was overpowering. I removed one cup of peas and blended them with some of the broth. After returning the blended peas to the soup, and another taste test, it was perfect.

HAM AND BEEF BONES

Ham and beef bones make an excellent broth. Cover with water and bring to a boil. Simmer for 30 minutes. Remove the bones and discard. Chill the broth and skim off all fat. The broth will store for one week in the refrigerator or will freeze well for about a month. Ham bone broth is especially good for bean soup.

COOKING SOUP IN A SLOW COOKER

Some soups lend themselves very well for a slow cooker. These include vegetable beef soup and steak soup. The cooking time will vary depending on your brand of slow cooker. The time can be four to six hours on high and as many as 12 hours on low.

HERBS

Five-spice powder

Allspice

Cayenne, hot sauce, powder,
  or flakes

Celery seeds

Chili powder

Cinnamon

Cloves

Coriander powder

Cumin

Curry powder

Dill weed

Fine herbs, see recipe on page 195

Garlic, garlic powder, garlic chips

Ginger

Marjoram

Mint

Mustard, dry

Nutmeg

Onion, instant

Paprika, sweet Hungarian

Parsley

Pickling spices

Rosemary

Sesame seeds

Sweet basil

Tarragon

Thyme

COOKING WITH HERBS

Cooking with herbs has two functions. They make things taste good and some are good for your health. It is the author's opinion that if you can taste an herb in a dish, you probably used too much. Herbs should blend together and not stand out over the taste of the food. There are some exceptions to this rule, however. Some herbs, like cinnamon, are meant to be tasted in some dishes. My fried banana recipe on page 149 is a good example.

FINE HERBS RECIPE

Many of the recipes in this book use fine herbs. These are expensive when purchased in small amounts at the store. You can make your own at a fraction of the cost. Blend equal parts of thyme, oregano, rosemary, and parsley. Mix well and store in a cool place out of the sunlight. Fine herbs work very well in soups and stews. Buy herbs and spices at the bulk food counter at the grocery store. Let me give you an example without naming any companies.

One company markets fine herbs, 1 ounce, that sells for $3.49. Another company markets a product named Italian Seasoning, $1^1/_4$ ounce, at $1.00, when purchased at a local discount store. The ingredients are identical. You can make the product for about fifty cents when purchased in bulk.

HEALTH AND HERBS

CAYENNE

It has been known for thousands of years that cayenne in any form (hot peppers, hot sauce or powder) can be used for treatment of digestive problems, for a toothache, or to ward off the chills at the onset of a cold.

Capraicin is the active ingredient in cayenne. When made into an ointment it can be used to relieve muscle and joint pain.

CINNAMON

Cinnamon has been known as a folk remedy for colds, flatulence, nausea, and vomiting. It can also be used to reduce stomach gases and to reduce diarrhea.

Cinnamon is derived from the bark of the cassia tree.

GARLIC

For centuries garlic has had magical powers for different cultures. It has been used as protection against vampires, to enhance sexual powers, and build up physical strength by the Egyptians. The Greeks used it as a laxative.

Today modern herbalists believe that garlic can be used as an effective herb to prevent colds, flu, and other infectious diseases. Recent research shows that garlic is effective in treating cardiovascular conditions. It is also effective in reducing high blood pressure.

GINGER

The Chinese have used ginger for over 2,000 years for treating colds, nausea, and seafood poisoning. Today, ginger tea is prescribed for stomach aches and to aid digestion. In addition, ginger is used to promote circulation and to reduce motion sickness.

ROSEMARY

Today rosemary is used to treat an upset stomach, aid digestive disorders, and reduce headaches. It is also used for circulatory disorders.

SUMMARY

We would be wise to take a lesson from the North American Indians who used wild plants and herbs to cure everything from coughs, colds, and diarrhea, to vomiting.

Using herbs to cook with can turn a dull, uninteresting dish into a work of art. The question always arises, "How much should I use?"

There are really no hard and fast rules to this question. It depends on an individual's taste. You will have to experiment to find your own comfort zone. I guess the old adage is really true. "Some like it hot, some like it not."

Happy Cooking,

Chef Dinosaur

INDEX